STECK–VAUGHN

# LIFE Skills

## FOR TODAY'S WORLD

### BY VIVIAN BERNSTEIN

*Personal Health*

D1519000

## CONSULTANTS

**Dee Marie Boydstun**
Literacy Coordinator
Black Hawk College
Moline, Illinois

**Marie S. Olsen**
Learning Center Coordinator
for Rio Salado Community College
at Maricopa Skill Center
Phoenix, Arizona

**John C. Ritter**
Teacher, Education Programs
Oregon Women's Correctional Center
Salem, Oregon

## STECK-VAUGHN
### COMPANY
A Subsidiary of National Education Corporation

## ABOUT THE AUTHOR

Vivian Bernstein is the author of *America's Story, World History and You, World Geography and You, American Government*, and *Decisions for Health*. She received her Master of Arts degree from New York University. Bernstein is active with professional organizations in social studies, education, and reading. She gives presentations to school faculties and professional groups about content area reading. Bernstein was a teacher in the New York City Public School System for a number of years.

## ACKNOWLEDGMENTS

*Executive Editor:* Diane Sharpe
*Project Editor:* Anne Souby
*Designer:* Pamela Heaney
*Photo Editor:* Margie Foster
*Production:* American Composition & Graphics, Inc.

## CREDITS

Cover Photograhy: © Tom McCarthy/PhotoEdit; (inset forms) Cooke Photographics

All photos by Park Street with the following exceptions.

p. 5 © Jean Higgins/Unicorn; p. 6 © Mark Burnett/PhotoEdit; p. 8 © Tony Freeman/PhotoEdit; p. 28 © A. Rodham/Unicorn; p. 35 © Tom McCarthy/Unicorn; p. 36 © Michael Newman/PhotoEdit; p. 38 Reagan Bradshaw; p. 56 © Custom Medical Stock; p. 59 © Custom Medical Stock; p. 60 © Amy C. Etra/PhotoEdit; p. 66 © Richard Hutchings/PhotoEdit; p. 70 © Amy C. Etra/PhotoEdit; p. 78 © Eric R. Berndt/Unicorn; p. 80 © Amy C. Etra/PhotoEdit.

Breast exam graphic reproduced with permission of the American Cancer Society.
Prescription labels reproduced with permission of Mitchell Gershowitz of Ocean Chemists.
Tylenol label reproduced with permission of Johnson & Johnson.
Hospital emergency room admission form reproduced with permission of South Nassau Communities Hospital.
Benadryl warning label reproduced with permission of Warner-Lambert Company.
Paint warning label reproduced with permission of The Glidden Company.

## ISBN 0–8114–1915–0

Printed in the United States of America.          **4 5 6 7 8 9 0     BP        98 97**

# CONTENTS

*Life Skills for Today's World* is a series of five books. These books are *Money and Consumers*, *The World of Work*, *Your Own Home*, *Personal Health*, and *Community and Government*. They can help you learn skills to be successful in today's world and will show you how to use these skills in your daily life.

This book is *Personal Health*. Each chapter in this book has six pages of lesson text. This text is followed by a workshop and exercises. One workshop in this book is "Completing a Medical History Form." What kind of medical forms have you filled out?

_____

_____

_____

In the "Thinking and Writing" exercise, you will be asked to write in your journal. Your journal can be a notebook or just a group of papers. Writing in a journal helps you gather your thoughts and put them on paper. One exercise in this book asks you to think about your health habits. You are asked to think about which ones are helping you and which ones are harming you. Thinking and writing about problems can help you find answers. Try it here. Think about questions or problems you may have about your health or safety. On the lines below, tell how you think this book will help you.

_____

_____

_____

There are an index, a glossary, and an answer key in the back of this book. These features can help you use this book independently.

Have fun working through this book. Then enjoy your new skills!

# Good Health Habits

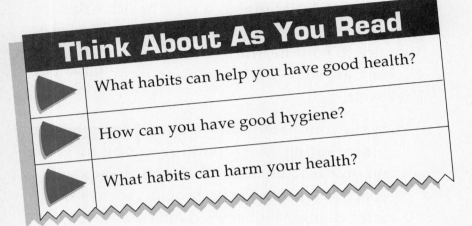

## Think About As You Read

What habits can help you have good health?

How can you have good hygiene?

What habits can harm your health?

Jennifer Brown is happy at her job. She likes the friends she has made at work. She also likes living in her new apartment. Jennifer knows that being healthy will allow her to enjoy life. She eats healthy meals and snacks. She keeps fit by playing sports a few times a week. Good health **habits** like these will help Jennifer stay well and enjoy life.

**Habits** are behaviors that people do often.

*Good health helps you enjoy life.*

## Protecting Your Health

Good health habits are habits that can protect your health. Brushing your teeth after meals is an example of a good health habit.

Poor health habits are habits that can damage your health. Nail biting is a poor health habit. Cigarette smoking is a habit that can cause great damage to your health.

Here are some health habits that can help you stay well.

1. Wash your hands with soap and warm water before eating. Most colds are caused by germs on unwashed hands. Wash your hands with soap after using the bathroom. Always wash after changing a baby's diaper.

2. Take care of your teeth. Brush them at least twice a day. It is best to brush after each meal. It takes about two minutes to brush your teeth correctly. **Floss** your teeth with dental floss each day. Visit a dentist for checkups every six months.

You **floss** when you clean between your teeth with a strong thread called dental floss.

*Practice good health habits.*

3. Get enough sleep. Your body repairs itself while you sleep. Most adults need about eight hours of sleep each night.

4. Practice good **posture**. Good posture shows that you feel good about yourself. Good posture keeps your body parts in the right places inside your body.

Your **posture** is the way you carry your body when you sit and stand.

5. Control your weight. Eat a healthy diet and exercise to control your weight. Try not to become too heavy or too thin.

6. Do something you enjoy each day. Choose an enjoyable activity to help you relax after a hard, busy day. You may enjoy listening to music, reading, visiting a friend, or having a hobby. Playing sports and exercising can also help you relax.

7. Protect yourself from the sun. The sun can damage your skin and cause skin **cancer**. Too much sun wrinkles your skin. Always wear a **sunscreen lotion** when you are outdoors. Use a lotion that has SPF15 or higher on the label. Many lotions work best if you use them thirty minutes before you go outside.

**Cancer** is a disease in which unhealthy cells attack and destroy the body's normal cells.

A **sunscreen lotion** blocks the sun's harmful rays from damaging your skin.

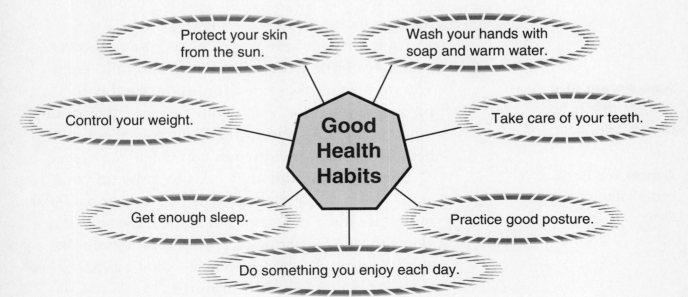

Protect your skin from the sun.

Wash your hands with soap and warm water.

Control your weight.

Take care of your teeth.

Good Health Habits

Get enough sleep.

Practice good posture.

Do something you enjoy each day.

*Keep your nails in shape.*

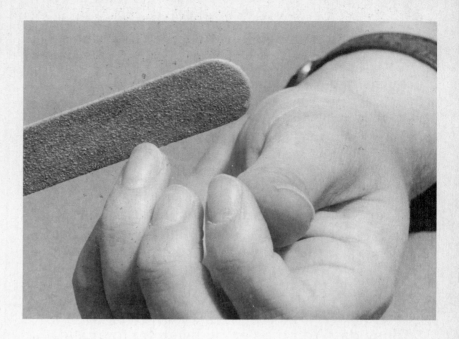

## Good Hygiene Habits

Your **hygiene** is the way you keep your body clean. Good hygiene habits help you look and feel your best.

To have good hygiene habits, take care of your hair, skin, and nails. Wash your hair with a mild shampoo. Wash your hair often to keep it looking clean and shiny.

Care for your nails by cleaning them with a small nail brush. Cut or file your nails to keep them looking nice.

Care for your skin by taking a bath or shower each day. Bathe with warm water and mild soap. You may want to use **deodorant** once a day to prevent body odor. Wash your face every morning when you get up and every night before going to bed. Brush your teeth when you wash your face.

Sometimes a **mole** may start to grow on your skin. Moles can be flat spots or raised bumps. Most moles are not a problem. But some moles become skin cancers. See a doctor if you have a mole that starts to grow or change in size, color, or shape. See a doctor if a mole bleeds or hurts.

The way you keep your body clean and healthy is called **hygiene**.

A **deodorant** is a product that is used to stop body odor.

A **mole** is a black or brown spot on the skin.

8

## Dangerous Health Habits

Cigarette smoking causes many illnesses and deaths each year. Cigarette smoking causes lung cancer. It causes heart and lung diseases. It also causes lip, throat, and mouth cancers. People who smoke become short of breath easily. It is harder for them to walk and run without feeling tired.

Cigarette smoking can harm the unborn babies of pregnant women. These babies are often smaller and less healthy than other babies. Cigarette smoke can also harm people who do not smoke.

If you do not smoke, try not to start. If you are a smoker, think about learning how to stop smoking. Talk to a doctor about your smoking habit. The doctor can suggest ways to help you stop smoking.

Drinking alcohol is another bad health habit. Beer, wine, and liquor are drinks that have alcohol in them. Alcohol is dangerous because it slows down the way your brain and your body work. You cannot think as clearly. You can get into accidents more easily. More than half of all car accidents are caused by drivers who have been drinking alcohol. It is against the law to drink and drive.

Try to find other ways of having fun with your friends rather than drinking alcohol. At parties drink soda, juice, or water instead of alcohol. If you do drink alcohol, know your limit.

**Drug abuse** is another dangerous habit. You abuse drugs by using medicines in ways that are not correct. You also abuse drugs by using **illegal** drugs like heroin, marijuana, and cocaine. Each year many people die because they abuse drugs. Choose friends who do not abuse drugs. Then you will not feel pressured to abuse drugs.

Having good health will help you enjoy life. Practicing good health habits will help you enjoy good health.

**Drug abuse** is the use of drugs in ways that are not correct or safe.

**Illegal** means against the law.

## Calling for a Medical Appointment

**G**ood health habits include visits to the doctor and dentist for checkups. You need an appointment to see a doctor or a dentist. Think about the time that you would want for your checkup. Then call for your appointment. A nurse or secretary will make the appointment when you call. He or she will ask for your name, address, home phone number, day phone number, and your age.

Jennifer Brown called Dr. Silver's office for an appointment. Read Jennifer's conversation with the nurse.

*Nurse:*     Doctor Silver's office.

*Jennifer:*     I'm calling to make an appointment.

*Nurse:*     Have you been here before?

*Jennifer:*     No. I'm a new patient.

*Nurse:*     What do you wish to see the doctor for?

*Jennifer:*     I want a complete checkup.

*Nurse:*     Which is better for you, morning or afternoon?

*Jennifer:*     I work during the day. I need an evening or a Saturday appointment.

*Nurse:*     We're not open in the evening or on Saturday.

*Jennifer:*     How late in the day do you take patients?

*Nurse:*     4:30 P.M.

*Jennifer:*     Then give me a 4:30 appointment, so I won't miss much work.

*Nurse:*     The earliest date I have is April 22.

*Jennifer:*     That's good. Put me down for that.

*Nurse:*     Okay. What is your full name and your age?

*Jennifer:*     I'm Jennifer Jean Brown. I'm 32.

| | |
|---|---|
| *Nurse:* | And your home phone number? |
| *Jennifer:* | 629-4300. |
| *Nurse:* | Do you have a phone number where you can be reached during the day? |
| *Jennifer:* | 432-9721. How much will my visit cost? |
| *Nurse:* | The cost depends on the tests the doctor does. Do you have insurance? |
| *Jennifer:* | Yes. I have group health insurance with my job. |
| *Nurse:* | We can accept your insurance as payment. We will file the form for you. Just be sure to bring your insurance card with you. |
| *Jennifer:* | Is there anything else I need to bring? |
| *Nurse:* | Bring a record of all your shots, if you have one. Any other questions? |
| *Jennifer:* | No. |
| *Nurse:* | Then we'll see you on Friday, April 22, at 4:30. Remember to call at least one day before if you cannot keep your appointment. |
| *Jennifer:* | Thank you. Good-bye. |

▼ ▼ ▼

**Answer these questions about Jennifer's conversation with the nurse.**

**1.** Why does Jennifer want to see the doctor? _____

**2.** When is Jennifer's appointment? _____

**3.** What does Jennifer have to bring to the doctor's office? _____

_____

**4.** What did the nurse tell Jennifer to do if she cannot keep the appointment?

_____

▶ **WORKSHOP PRACTICE: Make an Appointment**

Imagine you are calling to make an appointment with a
doctor named Dr. Sinclair. You want to see Dr. Sinclair
on May 5 at 4:30. Answer the questions the nurse
may ask you.

**1.** *Nurse:* Dr. Sinclair's office. Can I help you?
(State your reason for calling. Tell when you want the appointment.)

_____

_____

_____

**2.** *Nurse:* Dr. Sinclair can see you then. Tell me your name, age, home
phone number, and a daytime phone number.

(Write the information.) _____

_____

**3.** *Nurse:* Do you have any questions?

(What questions would you want to ask?) _____

_____

_____

_____

▶ **VOCABULARY:   Find the Meaning**
**On the line write the word or phrase that best completes each sentence.**

**1.** A disease in which unhealthy cells attack and destroy the body's normal

cells is _____ .

flu      cancer      common cold

**2.** Something that is _____ is against the law.

cheap      expensive      illegal

**3.** A _____ is a black or brown spot on the skin that can be dangerous if it starts to grow or change.

mole     nail     hair

**4.** The use of drugs in ways that are not correct or safe is

_____ .

drug abuse     hygiene     floss

**5.** To stop body odor, you would use _____ .

dental floss     deodorant     sunscreen lotion

## ▶ COMPREHENSION: Finish the Paragraph

**Use the following phrases to finish the paragraph.**
**Write the words you choose on the correct lines.**

smoking cigarettes          abusing drugs              drinking alcohol
practicing good posture     controlling your weight    washing your hands
sunscreen lotion            good health habits

Habits that help you stay well are _____ .

Three examples of good health habits are _____ ,

_____ , and _____

before eating. A good habit that helps you protect your skin from the sun is

using _____ . Avoid bad health habits like

_____ , _____ ,

and _____ .

**THINKING AND WRITING**   Think about your health habits. Which ones are helping you? Which ones may be harming you? How would you like to change your health habits? Explain your reasons in your journal.

# CHOOSING HEALTHY FOODS

## Think About As You Read

▶ Which types of food can be harmful to your health?

▶ What foods can you eat to protect your health?

▶ How can you save money when shopping for healthy foods?

People who weigh more than the correct weight for their age, height, and body frame are **overweight**.

**M**iguel Perez used to be **overweight**. He decided to change his poor eating habits to healthy ones. He learned to eat low-fat foods, less salt, and less sugar. He learned to eat more fruits, vegetables, and grains. Miguel slowly lost weight. Today he has the correct weight for his height and age. Miguel's new eating habits will help him have good health and not become overweight again.

*Choose fresh fruits and vegetables.*

*This meal is high in fat.*     *This meal is lower in fat.*

## Planning a Healthy Diet

You need food to give your body **calories** and **nutrients**. Calories give you the energy you need. Different foods have different amounts of calories. An orange has about 60 calories. Two small chocolate chip cookies have 130 calories.

Study the nutrient chart on page 16. By eating different foods, you will get the six nutrients your body needs.

Four types of foods can be harmful to your health.

1. Salty foods can cause high **blood pressure**. Salty chips, salty nuts, canned soups, smoked meat and fish, and lunch meats are very salty foods.

2. Some foods can raise the amount of **cholesterol** in your blood. High cholesterol can cause heart disease. Try to limit the amount of egg yolks, red meat, liver, and butter in your diet.

3. Fatty foods can lead to heart disease. They may cause some cancers. You need only a very small amount of fat in your diet. Some foods to avoid are whole milk, cream, chips, bacon, fried chicken, and hot dogs.

The energy we get from food is measured in **calories**.

**Nutrients** are six different substances in food that the body needs for health and life. The six nutrients are carbohydrates, proteins, fats, vitamins, minerals, and water.

**Blood pressure** is the pressure of the blood as it moves against the walls of the body's blood vessels. High blood pressure can lead to heart disease.

**Cholesterol** is a fatty substance in the blood. Too much cholesterol in the blood can cause heart disease.

# THE SIX KINDS OF NUTRIENTS YOUR BODY NEEDS

| Nutrient | How does the nutrient help your body? | What foods have this nutrient? |
|---|---|---|
| **❶ Carbohydrates** | | |
| Sugar | gives the body quick energy | white sugar, brown sugar, honey, syrup, candy, fruit |
| Starch | gives the body longer-lasting energy | potatoes, rice, cereals, corn, noodles, bread, sweet potatoes, barley, pasta |
| Fiber | helps the body remove wastes | fruits and vegetables with skins, whole grains (brown rice, oatmeal, whole-wheat bread), plain popcorn |
| **❷ Proteins** | help build muscles, bones, and teeth<br>help the body make new cells | meat, fish, chicken, eggs, turkey, milk, cheese, peanut butter, beans |
| **❸ Fats** | give the body energy<br>keep the body warm | butter, margarine, mayonnaise, chocolate bars, peanut butter, fatty meat, whole milk, whole-milk cheeses, cooking oils, chicken skin |
| **❹ Minerals** | | |
| Iron | helps red blood cells carry oxygen | red meat, beans, dark-green vegetables, whole grains |
| Calcium | helps build strong bones and teeth | milk, cheese, peas, beans, broccoli, spinach, green vegetables, salmon, sardines |
| **❺ Vitamins** | | |
| Vitamin A | helps you see in the dark<br>helps build healthy skin and teeth | carrots, green vegetables, fruits, butter, cream, whole milk, cheese |
| Beta-carotene | helps the body fight disease | sweet potatoes, carrots, cantaloupe, dark-green leafy vegetables |
| Vitamin $B_1$ | helps keep the brain and nerve cells healthy | brown rice, whole grains, cereals, milk, meat, fish, eggs, potatoes |
| Vitamin $B_2$ | helps keep the skin healthy | milk, cereal, whole grains, cheese, meat, eggs, fish, chicken |
| Vitamin C | helps keep skin, gums, and bones healthy | tomatoes, oranges, lemons, grapefruits, melons, potatoes, green vegetables |
| Vitamin D | helps build strong bones and teeth | eggs, milk, butter, fish, oils |
| **❻ Water** | helps the body digest food and get rid of wastes | water, milk, juice |

**16**

**4.** Foods with sugar can cause **tooth decay**. You can become overweight from eating too much sugar. Avoid candy, cakes, cookies, soda, and cereals that are high in sugar.

To lose weight, choose a low-fat diet that is also low in sugar, salt, and cholesterol. You want your diet to be high in **fiber**. Eat fruits, vegetables, and whole grains to get fiber and nutrients. These foods may protect you from heart disease and some cancers.

Study the Food Groups chart on page 18. Eat enough healthy foods from each food group every day.

## Controlling Your Weight

You look and feel your best when you are at your correct weight. It is not healthy to be too heavy or too thin. A doctor can tell you the weight that is correct for you.

You can gain weight if you eat more calories than your body uses for energy. The extra calories become fat in your body.

**Tooth decay** happens when acids in your mouth make a small hole on the surface of your tooth. The decay can destroy the tooth if it is not treated by a dentist.

**Fiber** is a carbohydrate from plants that helps the body remove wastes. The fiber in a food has no calories.

*Fruits and vegetables provide fiber and nutrients in your diet.*

# THE FOOD GROUPS

| Group | Foods in This Group | Foods to Avoid | Healthy Choices |
|---|---|---|---|
| ❶ **Grain Group** Eat 6 to 11 servings each day. | bread, cereal, pasta, rice, barley | sweet cereals, pasta in oily sauce, cakes, cookies | whole-wheat bread, whole-grain cereal, brown rice, bagels |
| ❷ **Fruit Group** Eat 2 to 4 servings each day. | all fruits, fruit juice | canned fruit in heavy syrup, fruit drinks made with sugar | different kinds of fresh fruits, fruit juice without added sugar |
| ❸ **Vegetable Group** Eat 3 to 5 servings each day. | all vegetables | fried vegetables | fresh salads; different kinds of fresh, frozen, or canned vegetables |
| ❹ **Meat-Nut-Eggs-Bean Group** Eat 2 to 3 servings each day. | chicken, turkey, meat, fish, eggs, peanut butter, canned beans, dried beans | smoked meats and fish, lunch meats with nitrites or nitrates, bacon, fatty meats, hot dogs, egg yolks, chicken skin, turkey skin, canned tuna in oil, fried fish | skinless chicken, turkey, egg whites, lean meat, small portions of baked or broiled fish, canned tuna in water |
| ❺ **Milk Group** Adults need 3 to 4 servings each day. Pregnant and nursing females need 4 to 5 servings each day. | milk, cheese, ice cream, yogurt | cream, butter, hard cheese, whole milk, ice cream | skim milk, 1% low-fat milk, nonfat and low-fat cheese, nonfat and low-fat ice cream and frozen yogurt |
| ❻ **Snack Group** Choose healthy snacks. Avoid sweet, fatty, and salty snacks. | fruit, raw vegetables, chips, candy, cookies, salted peanuts, pies, cake, pretzels, nuts | sweet, fatty, and salty snacks | fruit, raw vegetables, unbuttered popcorn, unsalted pretzels, rice cakes |

You lose weight if your body needs more calories than you get from your food. Then your body uses its own fat for energy, and you lose weight. Your body uses more calories when you exercise. So doing exercise may help you lose weight.

Check with your doctor before starting a diet. It is safe to lose one or two pounds a week. To keep weight off, eat low-fat meals and snacks.

## Buying Healthy Foods

Think about buying healthy foods each time you go to a food store. Buy healthy foods that family members will enjoy. Look for low-fat foods when you go food shopping.

Buy good-quality meat that is very lean. Be careful when buying hamburger meat. Some hamburger meats are very fatty. Hamburgers that are made from fatty meat become very small when they are cooked. Buy very lean meat for hamburgers.

Many adults and children like cereals. Sweet cereals are less healthy and more expensive. Try to buy cereals that do not have much sugar. You can sweeten the cereal with chopped fruit.

*Use fruit instead of sugar to sweeten your cereal.*

# CALORIES AND FATS IN FOODS

| Type of Food | Food | Calories | Fat (grams in a serving) |
|---|---|---|---|
| Meat, fish, or chicken | 1 small hamburger with bun | 250 | 10 |
| | 1 small fried chicken breast (with skin) | 364 | 19 |
| | 1 small roasted chicken breast (with skin) | 193 | 8 |
| | 1 small roasted chicken breast (without skin) | 142 | 3 |
| | 1 slice of bologna | 89 | 8 |
| | 2 ounces of canned tuna in water | 60 | 1 |
| | 2 ounces of canned tuna in oil | 150 | 10 |
| Milk and cheese | 1 cup of skim milk | 90 | less than 1 gram |
| | 1 cup of whole milk | 157 | 9 |
| | 1 ounce of American cheese | 105 | 9 |
| Snacks | 1 ounce of potato chips | 150 | 10 |
| | 1 ounce of pretzels | 120 | 2 |
| | 2 cups of plain popcorn | 60 | less than 1 gram |
| | 1 ounce of tortilla chips | 140 | 6 |
| | 1 chocolate candy bar | 240 | 14 |
| | 1 cup of ice cream | 270 | 14 |
| | 1 cup of nonfat frozen yogurt | 150 | 0 |
| Fruits and vegetables | 1 apple | 80 | 0 |
| | 1 orange | 62 | 0 |
| | 1 plain garden salad | 70 | 0 |
| | 1/2 cup of cooked broccoli | 25 | 0 |
| | 1 corn on the cob | 120 | 1 |
| | 1 baked potato | 220 | 0 |
| | 1 large serving of French fries | 285 | 14 |
| Baked foods | 2 slices of white bread | 140 | 2 |
| | 1 large bagel | 230 | 1 |
| | 1 chocolate-covered donut | 205 | 9 |
| | 2 small chocolate chip cookies | 130 | 5 |
| | 1 slice of chocolate cake with icing | 378 | 11 |

*Buying healthy food in bulk can save you money.*

There are other ways to save money when food shopping. Powdered milk is cheaper than fresh milk. Buy fresh fruits and vegetables during their growing season. Use canned or frozen fruits and vegetables when fresh ones are too expensive.

Save money and eat healthier foods by doing your own cooking. You can control the amount of sugar, salt, and fat in your food. Remove all chicken skin before cooking chicken. Let soups, sauces, and gravies cool off in the refrigerator. Then remove all fat that hardens on the top. Cut away all extra fat from meat before cooking it. Add salt only to foods that need it.

Large packages of food are often better buys. It may be cheaper to buy a five-pound bag of potatoes than to buy a few potatoes at a time. Buy large packages of food if you can use them.

Most of the calories in a healthy diet come from bread, cereal, **pasta**, and other grains. A healthy diet also has a lot of fruits and vegetables. These foods are much less expensive than meat, fish, and **poultry**. A small part of your calories can come from meat, fish, and poultry. Buying healthy foods can help you save money. Eating healthy foods will help you have good health.

Foods like macaroni, spaghetti, and noodles are **pasta**.

Birds that are used for their meat and eggs— such as turkeys, chickens, and ducks— are **poultry**.

## Reading Food Labels

Look at the food labels on page 23. Food labels help you learn the following facts about food.

**1** ▶ **Serving Size.** The information on the label is true for just one serving. The label tells you the serving size in weight. It also tells you how many servings are in the package.

**2** ▶ **Food Information.** It is important to know the amount of protein, carbohydrate, fat, cholesterol, and sodium in a food product. The amounts are given in grams (g) and in milligrams (mg). Sodium is a mineral found in salt. Sodium can raise your blood pressure. Most of the calories in a healthy diet need to come from the bread group. The bread group is high in carbohydrates. Limit fat, cholesterol, and sodium in your diet.

**3** ▶ **U.S. Recommended Daily Allowances.** The U.S. Recommended Daily Allowances (U.S. RDA) are the amounts of nutrients you need each day, according to the U.S. government. The label shows you what percent of each nutrient you get from this food. You need 100 percent of each nutrient each day.

**4** ▶ **Ingredients.** This is a list of foods that are used to make the product. The main ingredient is listed first. The ingredient used least is listed last.

▼ ▼ ▼

**Use both labels to answer the questions.**

**1.** The package of potato chips contains how many servings? _____

**2.** How many calories does one serving of pretzels have? _____

**3.** How many grams of fat does one serving of pretzels have? _____

**4.** How many grams of fat does one serving of potato chips have? _____

**5.** How much sodium is in one serving of potato chips? _____

**6.** What is the main ingredient in pretzels? _____

**7.** Which food supplies 10% of the U.S. RDA for Vitamin C? _____

## Unsalted Pretzels

NUTRITION INFORMATION
PER SERVING

**1** SERVING SIZE .........................1 ounce
SERVINGS PER CONTAINER ..........$9\frac{1}{2}$

**2** CALORIES .....................................120
PROTEIN ........................................3 g
CARBOHYDRATE .........................23 g
FAT ................................................2 g
CHOLESTEROL .........................0 mg
SODIUM ......................................5 mg
POTASSIUM ............................180 mg

**3** PERCENTAGE OF U.S. RECOMMENDED
DAILY ALLOWANCES (U.S. RDA)

PROTEIN............ 4    RIBOFLAVIN.......*
VITAMIN A.......... *   NIACIN...............*
VITAMIN C.......... *   CALCIUM............*
THIAMINE........... *   IRON...................2
*Contains less than 2 percent of the U.S.
RDA of these nutrients.

**4** INGREDIENTS: WHEAT FLOUR,
PARTIALLY HYDROGENATED VEG-
ETABLE OIL (MAY CONTAIN SOY-
BEAN OR COTTONSEED), CORN
SYRUP, POTASSIUM CHLORIDE,
BICARBONATES AND CARBONATES
OF POTASSIUM AND YEAST.

**Snack Foods, Inc.**
Phoenix, Arizona 85002

REG. PENNA. DEPT. AGR. (TPD)

# CRISPY Potato Chips

NUTRITION INFORMATION
PER SERVING

**1** Serving Size 1 ounce
Number of Servings 1

**2** Calories................................................150
Protein .................................................1 g
Carbohydrate ...................................15 g
Fat ......................................................10 g
Cholesterol† ....................................0 mg
Sodium ...........................................170 mg
Potassium ......................................380 mg

**3** PERCENTAGE OF U.S. RECOMMENDED
DAILY ALLOWANCES (U.S. RDA)

Protein ....................................................2
Vitamin A .................................................*
Vitamin C ..............................................10
Thiamine .................................................2
Riboflavin ................................................4
Niacin ......................................................4
Calcium ...................................................*
Iron ..........................................................2
† Information on fat and/or cholesterol
content is provided for individuals who, on
the advice of a physician, are modifying
their total dietary intake of fat and/or
cholesterol.

*Contains less than 2% U.S. RDA for
this nutrient.

**4** **Ingredients**: Potatoes, Vegetable Oil
(Contains one or more of the
following: Corn, Cottonseed, or
Partially Hydrogenated Soybean or
Sunflower Oil), and Salt.

No Preservatives.

**Dayton Foods, Inc.**
Chicago, Ill. 60608
Reg. Penna. Dept. Agr.

► **WORKSHOP PRACTICE: Compare Food Labels**

Look at the labels for potato chips and unsalted pretzels in the Life Skills Workshop on page 23. Answer these questions.

**1.** Which food has more carbohydrates? _____

**2.** Which food has more calories? _____

**3.** Which food is lower in sodium? _____

**4.** Which food is lower in fat? _____

**5.** Which food would you choose? _____

Why? _____

► **COMPREHENSION: Write the Answer**

**Write one or more sentences to answer each question.**

**1.** What are the six nutrients that come from food?

_____

_____

_____

**2.** What are four types of foods to avoid? Give two examples of each.

_____

_____

_____

_____

**3.** Doing exercise helps many people lose weight. Why?

_____

_____

_____

_____

**4.** What kinds of foods supply most of the calories in a healthy diet?

_____

_____

_____

**5.** How can buying healthy foods save you money?

_____

_____

_____

## VOCABULARY: Matching

**Match the word or phrase in Group B with a definition in Group A.**
**Write the letter of the correct answer on the line.**

### Group A

_____ **1.** These are the units used to measure the energy in food.

_____ **2.** This is the pressure of your blood as it moves against the walls of your blood vessels.

_____ **3.** This is a carbohydrate from plants that helps the body remove wastes.

_____ **4.** This type of food includes meat from chickens, turkeys, and ducks.

_____ **5.** Large amounts of this fatty substance in your blood can cause heart disease.

### Group B

**a.** fiber

**b.** cholesterol

**c.** poultry

**d.** calories

**e.** blood pressure

 **THINKING AND WRITING** Imagine that your doctor told you to lower the amount of fat, salt, and sugar in your diet. Which foods would you change? Which foods would you continue to eat although they are less healthy? Explain in your journal how you would change your diet.

# STAYING FIT AND HEALTHY

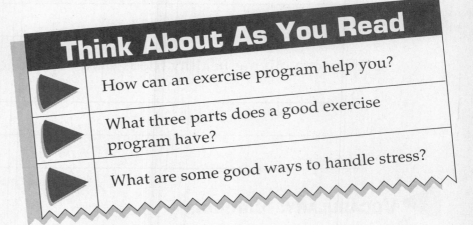

## Think About As You Read

▶ How can an exercise program help you?

▶ What three parts does a good exercise program have?

▶ What are some good ways to handle stress?

**R**oger Fields knew he needed more exercise. But it was hard for him to find time for it. He worked from 8:00 A.M. to 5:00 P.M. five days a week. He went to school two nights each week to get training for a better job. On other nights he helped his wife care for their children. Roger made time for exercise by getting up one hour earlier twice a week. He also exercised on weekends. His exercise program has helped him feel better.

*Exercise will help you stay fit.*

## How Exercise Helps Your Body

Each year more adults die from heart disease than from any other cause. An exercise program and a healthy diet can protect you from heart disease.

Exercise can help you in the following ways.

1. Exercise makes your heart and your **arteries** stronger.

2. Exercise helps lower the amount of cholesterol in the blood.

3. Exercise helps lower your blood pressure if it is too high.

4. Exercise helps you improve your posture. Good posture improves your appearance. It helps keep your heart, lungs, and stomach in the right places inside your body.

5. Exercise helps you control your weight.

6. Exercise helps lower **stress**. Most people feel happier and calmer after they exercise.

7. Exercise helps you have stronger bones. Stronger bones protect you from a disease called **osteoporosis**.

8. Exercise can help you have fun. You can enjoy activities like bike riding, swimming, and walking with your family and friends.

## Different Kinds of Exercise

There are different kinds of exercise. Each type can help you in a different way.

**Aerobic exercise** makes the heart stronger. Aerobic exercises include walking, running, jogging, and swimming. Other aerobic exercises are bike riding, jumping rope, and fast dancing. Walking up and down stairs is also an aerobic exercise.

Stretching exercises make your body more flexible. Then you can move and bend easily.

Your **arteries** are blood vessels that carry blood from your heart to different parts of your body.

**Stress** is the way the body responds to emotional, physical, and social pressures. Every person feels stress each day.

**Osteoporosis** is a disease in which the bones lose the mineral called calcium. This causes the bones to become weaker and break more easily.

An **aerobic exercise** uses repeated activity to make the heart work faster and make you breathe harder. It makes the heart stronger.

*Swimming is an exercise for people of all abilities.*

**Weight-bearing exercise** makes you push against weight to make your bones and muscles stronger.

A person with a **disability** finds it difficult to do certain things.

**Weight-bearing exercise** makes your bones and muscles stronger. Push-ups and lifting weights are two types of weight-bearing exercise.

Choose exercises and sports that you can enjoy throughout life. Walking, swimming, and bike riding are exercises for people of all ages. Tennis, ice skating, and hiking are other activities for all age groups.

Physical **disability** and illness may prevent you from doing certain types of exercise. But most people can do some types of exercise. Swimming is an exercise that most people can learn to do and enjoy.

You can develop a home exercise program for yourself. To strengthen your heart, plan to exercise at least three times a week. Your exercise program needs to have these three parts.

1. Warm-up. Allow 10 minutes to warm up your muscles. Stretch and bend to make your muscles less stiff.

**2.** Aerobic **workout**. Allow 20 to 30 minutes for aerobic exercise. Your workout will make your heart work faster. Bike riding, jumping rope, walking, or jogging are some of the activities you can do for your workout. Some people use video tapes to do aerobic dancing for their workout. These tapes also include warm-up and cool-down exercises.

A **workout** is a group of exercises that helps make the heart and the muscles stronger.

**3.** Cool-down. The cool-down helps your heart slow down. It helps your muscles relax. Allow 10 minutes for your cool-down. Slow walking and gentle stretching are good cool-down exercises.

It takes time to build strength and **endurance**. You may jog for 10 minutes your first week and 15 minutes your second week. By the third or fourth week, you may be able to jog for 20 minutes. Do not push yourself too hard. A good exercise program makes you feel a little tired. It should not make you so tired that you need to go to sleep when you are finished.

You have **endurance** when you can do activities, like jogging, for a long period of time.

## Your Three-Part Exercise Program

| The Warm-up | The Workout | The Cool-down |
| --- | --- | --- |

*Do 10 minutes of stretching.*

*Do one or more aerobic exercises for 20 to 30 minutes.*

*Do 10 minutes of stretching or slow walking.*

**29**

*Drink plenty of water when you exercise.*

An exercise program needs to be safe. These rules can help you exercise safely.

1. Have a checkup before starting an exercise program. You especially need a checkup if you plan to do more than walking for your aerobic workout.

2. Avoid drinking alcohol before you exercise.

3. Do not smoke for two hours before you exercise. Of course, it is best to stop smoking completely.

4. Do not exercise when you have a cold or a fever.

5. Exercise will make you sweat. Drink a large glass of water slowly after you finish exercising.

## Dealing with Stress

You have stress in your life each day. Getting to work on time causes some stress. Caring for a sick family member, losing your job, or not having enough money causes more stress.

Stress can harm your health. When you are under a lot of stress, your heart will beat faster. Your blood pressure will be higher. Your breathing will be faster. People who live with a lot of stress are more likely to have heart disease.

You cannot remove all stress in your life. But you can learn better ways to handle stress. Take care of your health by eating healthy foods and getting enough rest. Do an enjoyable activity each day.

An exercise workout helps you relax and lower stress. **Deep-breathing exercise** can also help you get rid of stress. One way to do deep breathing is to breathe in slowly through your nose. Count to eight silently. Then breathe out slowly to a count of eight. Do this many times to feel calmer.

Another way to handle stress is to learn to talk about your problems. Talk to a friend or family member that you trust. Try not to stay angry with other people.

To handle stress better, understand the cause of your stress. Try to change the cause if you can. Roger felt stress because the bus he took to work in the morning was often late. His boss said Roger would lose his job if he continued to be late. Roger solved this problem by taking an earlier bus to work. Even if this bus was late, Roger had plenty of time to get to his job by 8:00 A.M.

To look and feel your best, you need to be fit and healthy. Learning to handle stress will protect your health. A regular exercise program will help you stay fit and healthy.

**Deep-breathing exercise** is an exercise in which you take a deep breath, hold it, and then slowly breathe out. This exercise makes you feel calmer.

*Handle stress by taking time to do something you enjoy.*

# Planning an Exercise Program

To stay fit and healthy, you need to exercise at least three days each week. Your exercise program needs a warm-up, an aerobic workout, and a cool-down. Look at the two exercise programs Roger planned for himself.

| Roger's Indoor Exercise Program | Roger's Outdoor Exercise Program |
|---|---|
| **10 Minute Warm-up** <br> rolling head from side to side, touching toes, stretching arms above the head and to the sides, rolling the shoulders forward and backward, swinging arms from side to side, bending the knees up and down, bending at the waist from side to side | **10 Minute Warm-up** (to be done indoors or outdoors) <br> rolling head from side to side, touching toes, stretching arms above the head and to the sides, rolling the shoulders forward and backward, swinging arms from side to side, bending the knees up and down, bending at the waist from side to side |
| **20–30 Minute Workout** <br> • 10–15 minutes of jogging in place and 10 minutes of jumping rope <br> **or** <br> • 5–10 minutes of jumping rope and 20 minutes on an exercise bike | **20–30 Minute Workout** <br> Choose 1 activity: <br> • 30 minutes of fast walking <br> • 20 minutes of jogging <br> • 30 minutes of bicycle riding <br> • 30 minutes of swimming <br> • 30 minutes of skating |
| **10 Minute Cool-down** <br> Repeat warm-up exercises slowly. | **10 Minute Cool-down** <br> Walk slowly for 10 minutes. |

▼ ▼ ▼

**Answer the questions about Roger's exercise program.**

1. What are some of Roger's warm-up exercises? _____

_____

2. What can Roger do for an indoor workout? _____

_____

3. What can Roger do for an outdoor workout? _____

_____

4. What can Roger do for his cool-down? _____

_____

▶ **WORKSHOP PRACTICE: Plan an Exercise Program**

Look back at Roger's exercise program in the Life Skills
Workshop. Use it as a guide to plan your own exercise
program. Write which exercises you would do for your
warm-up, workout, and cool-down.

| **Indoor Exercise Program** | **Outdoor Exercise Program** |
|---|---|
| **1.** Warm-up | **1.** Warm-up |
| | |
| **2.** Workout | **2.** Workout |
| | |
| **3.** Cool-down | **3.** Cool-down |

▶ **COMPREHENSION: True or False**

**Write True next to each sentence that is true. Write False next to
each sentence that is false. There are two false sentences.**

_____ **1.** Exercise can help prevent heart disease and osteoporosis.

_____ **2.** Jogging is a good cool-down exercise.

_____ **3.** Exercise can lower your blood pressure and your blood cholesterol.

_____ **4.** Two good ways to handle stress are to talk about your problems and to do an activity you enjoy.

_____ **5.** You must exercise every day to make your heart stronger.

**On the lines that follow, rewrite the two false sentences to make them true.**

_____

_____

## VOCABULARY: Finish the Sentence

**Choose one of the following words or phrases to complete each sentence. Write the word or phrase on the correct line.**

osteoporosis
stress
arteries
endurance
aerobic exercise

**1.** _____ is the way the body responds to emotional, physical, and social pressures.

**2.** Your body has developed _____ when you can do activities like running and jogging for a long period of time.

**3.** The disease in which bones lose calcium and become weak is called _____ .

**4.** Your _____ are blood vessels that carry blood from your heart to different parts of your body.

**5.** _____ uses repeated activity to make the heart work faster and become stronger.

**THINKING AND WRITING** Think about the ways you handle stress. Do you think you manage stress well? Explain in your journal how you handle stress. Tell why you do or do not handle stress well. Then tell how you can improve the way you handle stress.

# CARING FOR YOUR HEALTH

## Think About As You Read

▶ What kinds of medical tests can help you find cancer early?

▶ What are the seven warning signs of cancer?

▶ What are some good health habits that can help you stay well?

Joe Moore had a complete checkup when he started his new job in a hospital. During the checkup the doctor checked Joe's blood pressure. Joe was surprised to learn he had high blood pressure. The doctor told Joe to lower his blood pressure by eating a low-salt diet. Joe was told to walk for thirty minutes each day. The doctor told Joe to have his blood pressure checked again in two months. By taking care of his problem, Joe could protect his health.

*Have your blood pressure checked at least once a year.*

## Taking Care of Your Health with Checkups

Before the age of forty you need a complete checkup once in five years. People between the ages of forty and fifty need to be checked every other year. People who are more than fifty need a checkup every year.

The chart on page 37 shows the medical tests you may need. These tests can help your doctor find health problems before they become dangerous diseases.

Doctors have learned to make special medicines called **vaccines**. Young children need many vaccines before they start school. The chart on page 37 shows some vaccines that adults also need.

Have your eyes checked once in two years. Have your eyes checked for **glaucoma** after you are 35. Usually you will have no pain in your eyes if you have glaucoma. Only your eye doctor can tell. You can become blind if you have glaucoma and do not take care of it.

## Understanding Cancer

There are many different kinds of cancers. Some common cancers are lung cancer, breast cancer, and skin cancer.

**Vaccines** are medicines that protect you from getting certain diseases.

**Glaucoma** is an eye disease in which pressure inside the eye can cause blindness.

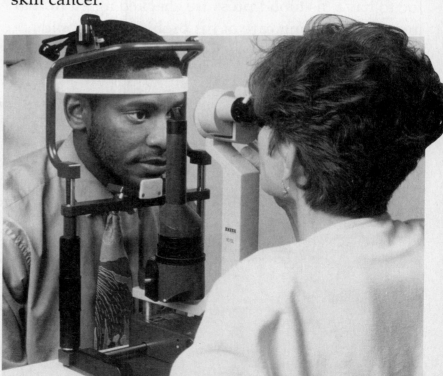

*Have your eyes checked for glaucoma.*

## MEDICAL TESTS AND VACCINES

| Test or Vaccine | How Can This Test or Vaccine Help You? | When Should This Be Done? |
|---|---|---|
| ❶ blood pressure test | Control high blood pressure so it does not cause heart disease. | once a year |
| ❷ routine blood tests | Find and treat different kinds of health problems early. | every three years |
| ❸ cholesterol blood test | You can lower your cholesterol level to protect yourself from heart disease. | once in three years |
| ❹ blood tests for AIDS and STDs (sexually transmitted diseases) | Find out if you have one of these diseases. Use available treatments. Avoid spreading the disease to others. | once a year if you have intimate sexual behavior with more than one partner |
| ❺ breast examination by a doctor | Doctors can treat or remove small breast lumps before they become dangerous cancers. | once a year |
| ❻ mammography (breast x-rays for women) | Find and treat very tiny breast cancers before they spread throughout the body. | Have one at age 35. Then every other year after age 40. Then every year after age 50. |
| ❼ Pap smear for women | Doctors can find and treat cervical cancer early. | once a year |
| ❽ test for hidden blood in the bowels | Find and treat colon cancer early. | once a year after age 40 |
| ❾ rectal exam | Find and treat colon cancer early. | once a year after age 40 |
| ❿ tetanus/diphtheria booster shot | Prevent the diseases of tetanus and whooping cough. | once in ten years |
| ⓫ rubella vaccine | Prevent pregnant women from getting German measles since it can harm their babies. | All nonpregnant women should get the shot. |
| ⓬ glaucoma eye test | Glaucoma causes blindness. Treat it early to prevent blindness. | every other year after age 35 |

*Smoking can cause many health problems.*

A **tumor** is a lump that can grow anywhere in the body. A tumor can be made of normal cells or cancer cells.

A **wart** is a small lump on the skin that is caused by a virus.

The intestine is called a **bowel**. Solid waste leaves your body when you have a bowel movement.

Your **bladder** holds liquid waste, or urine, until it leaves the body.

**Discharge** is a liquid that comes out of the body.

Cancer cells often form a lump called a **tumor**. Sometimes cancer cells break away from the tumor and travel to other parts of the body. Then these cancer cells destroy normal cells in those parts of the body. Each year many people die from cancer that has spread throughout the body.

Cancer can be treated and cured. To be cured, cancer must be found early. It must be treated before it has spread throughout the body.

The American Cancer Society tells people to look for these seven warning signs of cancer. See your doctor if any of these warning signs lasts longer than two weeks.

1. A sore on any part of the body that does not heal.

2. A small or large lump in the breast or any part of the body.

3. A mole or **wart** that changes in size, shape, or color.

4. A cough or a hoarse voice that lasts more than two weeks.

5. A change in your **bowel** or **bladder** habits.

6. Unusual bleeding or **discharge**.

7. Difficulty in swallowing or a sick feeling in your stomach after eating food.

You can also protect yourself from cancer in seven ways. First, do not smoke. Second, avoid drinking alcohol. Third, eat a low-fat diet. Fourth, eat fruits, vegetables, and cereals that are high in fiber. Fifth, avoid breathing dangerous chemicals. Sixth, protect your skin from the sun with sunscreen lotion. Seventh, learn how to **examine** yourself for lumps. Ask your doctor to show you how. Check for changes in warts and moles. Women need to check their breasts once a month. Men between the ages of 15 and 34 need to check their **testes** once a month.

To **examine** means to study and check something carefully.

**Testes** are male sex organs.

## Caring for Your Health

Every year millions of people get sick with the common cold. Medicines do not cure colds. Resting and drinking liquids will help you feel better faster. Throw away all used tissues because they can spread cold germs to others.

Use good health habits to protect your health. Bathe or shower daily. Wash your hands before eating. Learn to handle stress. Build good relationships with your family and friends. All of these habits will help you stay well.

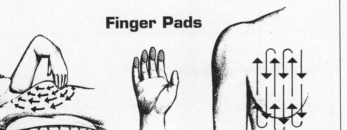

**Finger Pads**

**FEEL FOR:**
- lumps
- thickness
- other changes

**ONCE A MONTH:**
- Check each breast all over
- Check under your armpit too
- Use your finger pads
- Go up and down

American Cancer Society

*Women need to check their breasts each month.*

## Completing a Medical History Form

**Y**ou will be asked to complete a medical history form during your first visit to a doctor. This form helps the doctor learn about any health problems you may have. Be honest when you complete the medical history form. The information that you write down will be used to help you.

Look at the medical history form that Joe Moore completed when he visited a new doctor. Notice the following parts.

**1** ▶ **General.** This part asks why you are seeing the doctor now. You also tell what medicines you are using. Write down what allergies to medicine you have. A medicine allergy means the medicine gives you a rash or it makes you sick in some way.

**2** ▶ **Personal/Social.** This part asks about your health habits. The doctor wants to know how healthy you are.

**3** ▶ **Current History.** You tell about the health problems you are having right now.

**4** ▶ **Past History.** This section asks about your past health history. Write down past illnesses and injuries that lasted more than a week.

▼ ▼ ▼

**Answer these questions about Joe Moore's medical history form.**

**1.** What does Joe feel are his health problems? _____

**2.** What medicines does Joe take? _____

**3.** What medicine is Joe allergic to? _____

**4.** What is causing stress in Joe's life? _____

_____

**5.** What is Joe's health problem now? _____

_____

**6.** What caused Joe to miss more than a week of work? _____

# ADULT HEALTH HISTORY

Date *March 30, 1994*

Name *Joe Moore*  Date of Birth *June 13, 1967*  Record # _____

NOTE: This form will provide your physician and nurse with basic information about your health care background and needs. Please be as complete as possible. Also, if you do not understand a question or term, please ask for assistance.

## 1 GENERAL

- What do you feel are your health problems? *asthma*

- What prescribed and non-prescribed medications do you take? *Vanceril inhaler, Proventil inhaler*

- Do you have any medication allergies? Please list. *penicillin*

## 2 PERSONAL/SOCIAL

- Occupation *hospital maintenance worker*
- Are you   Single ___✓___   Married _____   Divorced _____ ?   Number of Children _____
- Is your diet healthful?        ✓Yes ___No        • Do you exercise regularly?        ✓Yes ___No
- Do you use seatbelts?        ✓Yes ___No        • Do you feel your life is stressful?        ✓Yes ___No
- Do you smoke?        ___Yes ✓No
- Do you drink and/or use drugs?        ___Yes ✓No        If Yes, how much *I do not earn enough money + I worry about my father since he had a heart attack.*

If Yes, check amount:   rarely _____   socially _____

moderately _____   excessively _____

## 3 CURRENT HISTORY

- Are you presently suffering from problems of:

| | | |
|---|---|---|
| breathing ___Yes ✓No | hearing ___Yes ✓No | bleeding from bowels ___Yes ✓No |
| digestion ___Yes ✓No | vision ___Yes ✓No | thyroid disease ___Yes ✓No |
| arthritis ___Yes ✓No | diabetes ___Yes ✓No | heart disease ___Yes ✓No |
| urination ___Yes ✓No | sex organs ___Yes ✓No | menstrual periods ___Yes ✓No |
| headaches ___Yes ✓No | dizziness, fainting ___Yes ✓No | other ✓Yes ___No |

- If any of the above are Yes, please explain *I cough for days after I have an asthma attack.*

## 4 PAST HISTORY

- Have you ever been exposed to chemicals or other harmful substances at work or elsewhere? If Yes, please explain *no*

- Did you have radiation treatments as a child? ___Yes ✓No

- Did your mother take hormones while she was pregnant with you? ___Yes ✓No

- Have you lost more than a week from work or school due to illness or injury? ✓Yes ___No

If Yes, please explain *flu in January*

## PAST HISTORY

- Have you ever been hospitalized? ___✓___ Yes _____ No

If Yes, please list date(s) and reason(s) for hospitalization ___1984, appendectomy___

- Have you had any other serious injury or illness such as tuberculosis or rheumatic fever which required a doctor's care in the past? _____ Yes ___✓___ No

If Yes, please list injury/illness and date it occurred _____

- Were you immunized in childhood or military service? ___✓___ Yes _____ No
- Has 10 years passed since your last tetanus booster? ___✓___ Yes _____ No    Date received ___1980___
- Are you immune to rubella? ___✓___ Yes _____ No

- Has any member of your family had:

| | | | | | |
|---|---|---|---|---|---|
| diabetes? | _____ Yes | ✓ No | kidney disease? | _____ Yes | ✓ No |
| high blood pressure? | ✓ Yes | _____ No | gallstones? | _____ Yes | ✓ No |
| heart disease? | ✓ Yes | _____ No | tuberculosis? | _____ Yes | ✓ No |
| cancer, of the breast? | _____ Yes | ✓ No | alcoholism? | _____ Yes | ✓ No |
| of the colon? | _____ Yes | ✓ No | suicide? | _____ Yes | ✓ No |
| other cancer? | _____ Yes | ✓ No | mental illness? | _____ Yes | ✓ No |
| glaucoma? | ✓ Yes | _____ No | aneurysm? | _____ Yes | ✓ No |
| arthritis? | ✓ Yes | _____ No | seizures? | _____ Yes | ✓ No |

## FAMILY HISTORY

| FAMILY MEMBER | IF DECEASED, AGE AT AND CAUSE OF DEATH | IF LIVING, AGE AND HEALTH PROBLEMS |
|---|---|---|
| mother | | 46, high blood pressure |
| father | | 50, heart attack in 1992 |
| maternal grandmother | | 74, high blood pressure |
| maternal grandfather | | 76, glaucoma |
| paternal grandmother | | 72, arthritis |
| paternal grandfather | 73, heart attack | |
| other family member with significant illness(es)  brother | | 31, asthma and high blood pressure |

In planning for your future health care, we would like to know what extra health services you feel you might want or need. In addition to caring for you when you are sick, what else would you like your physician to do for you?

Help me develop a good diet and exercise program. Help me manage my asthma better so I will get fewer attacks.

___Joe Moore___
Patient Signature

**5 ▶ Past History, continued.** Write down the times you spent in the hospital. Know when you had all your vaccine shots. Joe needs a tetanus booster since he has not had one in ten years. Tetanus is a disease you can get from germs that enter your body through a break in the skin. These germs live in dirt. A tetanus shot will keep you from getting tetanus. If you are immune to rubella, you have had German measles and cannot get it again.

**6 ▶ Family History.** Many diseases run in families. The information you give your doctor may help him or her find and treat a problem before you become very sick. "Deceased" means that someone has died. Your maternal grandparents are your mother's parents. Your paternal grandparents are your father's parents.

**7 ▶ Your Needs.** The doctor will care for you when you are sick. Tell what else you want from the doctor to help you with your health.

▼ ▼ ▼

**Answer these questions about Joe Moore's medical history form.**

**7.** When and why was Joe in the hospital?

_____

**8.** What health problems have Joe's family members had?

_____

_____

_____

**9.** What else does Joe want the doctor to help him with?

_____

_____

_____

**43**

## ▶ WORKSHOP PRACTICE: Complete a Medical History Form

Fill out the Family History part of the medical history form on this page. Keep this information. Take it with you when you visit your doctor. Use it to help you complete the medical history form at your doctor's office. Use the Life Skills Workshop as a guide.

**FAMILY HISTORY**

• Has any member of your family had:

| | | | | |
|---|---|---|---|---|
| diabetes? | _____ Yes _____ No | kidney disease? | _____ Yes _____ No |
| high blood pressure? | _____ Yes _____ No | gallstones? | _____ Yes _____ No |
| heart disease? | _____ Yes _____ No | tuberculosis? | _____ Yes _____ No |
| cancer, of the breast? | _____ Yes _____ No | alcoholism? | _____ Yes _____ No |
| of the colon? | _____ Yes _____ No | suicide? | _____ Yes _____ No |
| other cancer? | _____ Yes _____ No | mental illness? | _____ Yes _____ No |
| glaucoma? | _____ Yes _____ No | aneurysm? | _____ Yes _____ No |
| arthritis? | _____ Yes _____ No | seizures? | _____ Yes _____ No |

| FAMILY MEMBER | IF DECEASED, AGE AT AND CAUSE OF DEATH | IF LIVING, AGE AND HEALTH PROBLEMS |
|---|---|---|
| mother | | |
| father | | |
| maternal grandmother | | |
| maternal grandfather | | |
| paternal grandmother | | |
| paternal grandfather | | |
| other family member with significant illness(es) | | |

## ▶ COMPREHENSION: Circle the Answer
**Draw a circle around the correct answer.**

**1.** How often does your blood pressure need to be checked?

every year      once in two years      once in five years

**2.** How often do women need to check their breasts for lumps?

once a week      once a month      once a year

**3.** When is it very hard to cure cancer?

when cancer is found early

when tumors are very small

when cancer cells have spread throughout the body

**4.** How long do you need to wait before seeing a doctor if you have one of the seven warning signs of cancer?

three days     two weeks     two months

**5.** What is the best way to treat a cold?

take medicine     do exercise     rest and drink liquids

 **VOCABULARY:** Writing with Vocabulary Words
**Use six or more of the following words to write a paragraph that tells how you can care for your health.**

vaccines
tumors
cancer
bowel
wart
bladder
discharge
examine
glaucoma

_____

_____

_____

_____

_____

_____

_____

_____

 **THINKING AND WRITING** Read on page 39 about the seven ways you can protect yourself from cancer. What changes in your health habits would you want to make to protect your health? In your journal explain what changes you would make. Then tell how and why you would make these changes.

# CROSSWORD PUZZLE: Health and Happiness

Use the clues below to complete the crossword puzzle on page 47.
Choose from the words listed on page 47.

## Across

2. A _____ is a small lump on the skin that is caused by a virus.

4. Too much _____, a fatty substance in the blood, can cause heart disease.

5. You have _____ when you can do activities, like jogging, for a long period of time.

7. Your _____ is the way you carry your body when you sit and stand.

11. The way the body responds to emotional, physical, and social pressures is called _____ .

12. Your _____ are blood vessels that carry blood from your heart to different parts of your body.

## Down

1. Medicines that protect you from getting certain diseases are _____ .

3. _____ is an eye disease in which pressure inside the eye can cause blindness.

6. The energy we get from food is measured in _____ .

8. To _____ means to study and check something carefully.

9. A disease in which unhealthy cells attack and destroy the body's normal cells is _____ .

10. A _____ is a group of exercises that helps make the heart and the muscles stronger.

arteries     endurance     stress

calories     examine     vaccines

cancer     glaucoma     wart

cholesterol     posture     workout

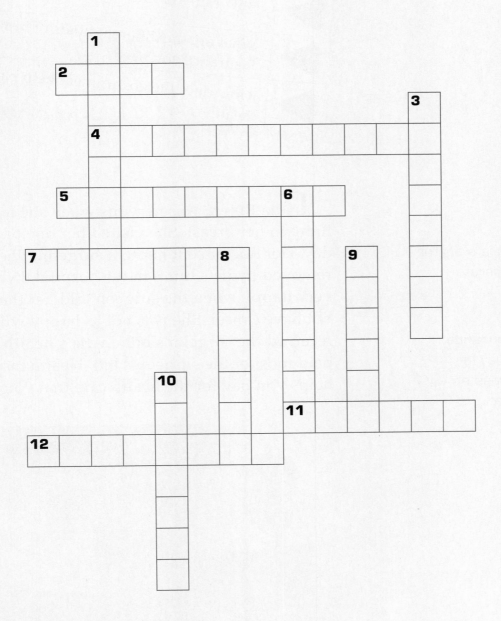

# HEALTH CARE

## Think About As You Read

▶ How can you find a good doctor?

▶ What are the different kinds of health insurance you need?

▶ How does the government help pay for health care?

A **surgeon** is a doctor who can operate.

**Health insurance** helps you pay for different types of health care.

Lydia Rivera was nervous when she found a lump in her breast. She visited her doctor the next day. Her doctor sent her to a **surgeon**. The surgeon removed Lydia's lump in the hospital. Lydia was very happy when the surgeon told her that she did not have cancer. She was not as happy when she received the surgeon's bill. Lydia's **health insurance** paid most of the surgeon's bill. Health insurance helps you pay for the health care that you need.

*Health insurance can help you pay medical bills.*

Many people buy group health insurance. Group plans cost less than private plans. Group plans may be provided through the company where you work. As long as you work for the company, you can have the group health insurance plan. If you leave your job, you may lose your group insurance.

Some people buy private health insurance plans. These plans are very expensive. Compare the price of a few plans from different insurance companies. Choose the plan that gives you the best protection and the best price.

## Other Ways to Pay for Health Care

You may want to join a **Health Maintenance Organization**, or **HMO**, to pay less for your health care. You will pay a fee to be a member of the HMO. That fee allows you to get all the medical care you need for the year. The fee will pay for medical tests, doctor visits, surgery, and hospital stays. But you have to use HMO doctors and hospitals. If you go to a doctor or hospital that is not part of the HMO, you will have to pay the bills yourself.

The government also helps people pay for medical care. All people who are 65 years or older can receive **Medicare** insurance. Younger people with disabilities can sometimes receive Medicare. Medicare helps people pay for hospital stays and doctor bills. Sign up for Medicare at a social security office near your home.

**Medicaid** is another government health insurance program. It is for people with low incomes. Medicaid pays for hospital costs, medicine, tests, and doctor bills. Call the health and welfare office near your home to apply for Medicaid.

Every person needs health insurance. If you have health insurance now, find out more about it. Learn what it will and will not cover. If you do not have insurance, try to buy some kind of health plan that you can afford. You need an insurance plan that will pay for good health care when you need it.

A **Health Maintenance Organization (HMO)** is a group of doctors and hospitals that have agreed to provide medical services at a special rate to their members.

**Medicare** is a government health insurance program that pays for hospital stays for people who are at least 65 years old. Some disabled people can get Medicare.

**Medicaid** is a government health insurance program to provide health care for people with low incomes.

# Completing a Health Insurance Form

**E**ach time you see a doctor, you will complete a health insurance form. When you mail it to your health insurance company, the company will pay you back for part of your bill. Some doctors will send in the form for you. Then the insurance company will pay your bill by sending a check to your doctor.

Lydia Rivera took her son to the doctor. She completed the health insurance form on page 53. Notice the following parts.

**1** **Employee and Dependent Information.** The first name to list is the owner of the insurance plan. A **dependent** is a person whose living expenses are paid by an adult. A child is the dependent of the parents. If the doctor visit is for a dependent, fill out that part. If the owner of the insurance is also the patient, then the dependent part would be left blank. Fill in employment information for other family members.

**2** **Accident Information.** Complete this part if the patient had an accident. Insurance plans almost always pay for the total medical costs of accidents.

**3** **Other Coverage Information.** Perhaps another family member has group health insurance with another job. Your insurance company will pay part of the bill. The other company will pay the rest.

**4** **Itemized Bills.** Your doctor may give you a bill or bills listing all the expenses of your visit. Those bills need to be sent in with this form.

▼ ▼ ▼

**Use Lydia's insurance form to answer the following questions.**

**1.** Who is Lydia's dependent? _____

**2.** Where does Lydia's husband work? _____

**3.** Why did Jesse visit the doctor? _____

**4.** What other health insurance company covers Lydia's family?

_____

**AMERICAN** health insurance

Statement of Claim for
Medical Expense Benefits

## Employee's Statement

**Answer all questions below.
Omitted information will cause delays.**

**1**

| Name (print) First Middle Last | Social Security Number | Date of Birth | ☐ Male |
|---|---|---|---|
| Lydia M. Rivera | 092 36 7653 | 2/21/60 | ☑ Female |

| Present Address: Street City State Zip Code | Marital ☐ Single ☐ Widowed | Telephone No. |
|---|---|---|
| 609 East 7th Ave. Chicago IL 60629 | Status: ☑ Married ☐ Divorced | (312) 555-4411 Area Code |

**Dependent Information** — Complete this section only if expenses were incurred by an eligible dependent or dependents.

| Name (print) First Middle Last | Social Security Number | If dependent (other than spouse) is over age 18 answer the following: |
|---|---|---|
| Jesse C. Rivera | 122/78/1529 | ☐ Disabled |

| Date of Birth | Relationship | ☑ Male ☐ Female | Marital ☑ Single | ☐ Student: No. of Units_____ |
|---|---|---|---|---|
| 11/14/89 | son | | Status: ☐ Married | |

**Family Employment** — Complete this section only if other members, including dependent minors, are employed.

| Name of Family Member (print) First Middle Last | Relationship | Date of Birth | Employer's Telephone No. |
|---|---|---|---|
| Carlos R. Rivera | husband | 7/14/59 | (312) 555-1100 Area Code |

| Employer's Name (print) | Employer's Address — Street City State Zip Code |
|---|---|
| Central Animal Hospital | 40 Orchard St. Chicago IL 60609 |

**2**

**Accident Information** — Complete this section only if claim is result of accidental injury or occupational sickness.

| Date of Accident | Time of Accident ☐ A.M. ☑ P.M. | Where Did the Accident Occur? (City, State) | Did the Accident/Sickness Happen at Work? ☐ Yes ☑ No |
|---|---|---|---|
| 2/2/94 | 7:00 | 609 East 7th Ave, Chicago, Il | |

Describe Accident or Occupational Sickness
Jesse slipped on a wet floor and turned his ankle.

**Medicare Information** — Complete this section only if Patient is eligible for Medicare.

| Please Attach a Copy of the "Explanation of Benefits" Statement From Your Medicare Insurance Carrier. | | Part A | Effective Date | Part B | Effective Date |
|---|---|---|---|---|---|
| | Medicare | | | | |

**3**

**Other Coverage Information** — This section must always be completed.

Are any benefits or services provided under another group insurance plan or any prepayment plan, or pursuant to any law (Federal, State, or Local) on account of the treatment reported on this claim?

☑ Yes ☐ No

If "Yes," answer (A) or (B), whichever applies, and (C).

A. Other Insurance Coverage is: ☑ Group ☐ Individual
☐ Other (specify) ➤ All American Insurance

B. Name or Type of Law is (e.g., Medicaid, Champus, No-Fault)

C. Give Name and Address of Other Company or Organization Providing Benefits or Services.

Name All American Insurance
Address 999 W. Broadway
City Chicago State IL Zip Code 60613

Please Indicate Plan Identification No. or Group No.(s). ➤ 7836576

**4**

**Itemized Bills** — Attach itemized bills for expenses not reported on this form. All such miscellaneous bills must show:

a. Employee's Name   b. Patient's Name (if not employee)   c. Name and Address of Provider of Services   d. Diagnosis

e. Complete Description of Services Rendered   f. Initials of Attending or Prescribing Physician   g. Dates (month, day, year) of Service

### Certifications and Medical Authorization

I authorize any insurance company, organization, employer, hospital, physician, or pharmacist to release any information requested with regard to this claim and the expenses reported.
I certify that the information I furnish in support of this claim is true and correct. I know it is a crime to fill out this form with facts I know are false or to leave out facts I know are important.

Signed (Employee)
*Lydia M. Rivera* Date 2/2/94

Signed (Dependent patient, not minor)

Date

### Payment of Benefits

I hereby authorize payment of benefits otherwise payable to me up to the stated charges to the provider(s) of services for all bills included with this statement — unless otherwise noted.

I understand I am financially responsible for any amounts not payable or not covered by the plan.

Signed (Employee)

*Lydia M. Rivera* Date 2/2/94

▶ **WORKSHOP PRACTICE:** Complete a Health Insurance Form

Practice filling out a health insurance form. Complete the sections below. Keep this page. Use it as a guide whenever you need to complete a health insurance claim. Use the Life Skills Workshop on pages 52–53 to help you complete this form.

Statement of Claim for
Medical Expense Benefits

| Employee's Statement | Answer all questions below. Omitted information will cause delays. |
|---|---|

| Name (print)   First   Middle   Last | Social Security Number / / | Date of Birth | ☐ Male ☐ Female |
|---|---|---|---|

| Present Address:   Street   City   State   Zip Code | Marital ☐ Single   ☐ Widowed Status: ☐ Married   ☐ Divorced | Telephone No. ( ) Area Code |
|---|---|---|

**Family Employment** — Complete this section only if other members, including dependent minors, are employed.

| Name of Family Member (print)  First   Middle   Last | Relationship | Date of Birth | Employer's Telephone No. ( ) Area Code |
|---|---|---|---|

| Employer's Name (print) | Employer's Address — Street   City   State   Zip Code |
|---|---|

**Other Coverage Information** — This section must always be completed.

| Are any benefits or services provided under another group insurance plan or any prepayment plan, or pursuant to any law (Federal, State, or Local) on account of the treatment reported on this claim? ☐ Yes   ☐ No If "Yes," answer (A) or (B), whichever applies, and (C). | C. Give Name and Address of Other Company or Organization Providing Benefits or Services. Name |
|---|---|
| A. Other Insurance Coverage is:  ☐ Group  ☐ Individual ☐ Other (specify) ➤ | Address City   State   Zip Code |
| B. Name or Type of Law is (e.g., Medicaid, Champus, No-Fault) | Please Indicate Plan Identification No. or Group No.(s). ➤ |

▶ **COMPREHENSION:** Write the Answer

**Write one or more sentences to answer each question.**

**1.** How can you find a good doctor?

_____

_____

_____

**2.** What three kinds of health insurance do people need?

_____

_____

_____

3. Why do many people buy group health insurance instead of private health insurance?

_____

_____

4. Why do many people join an HMO?

_____

_____

5. What is the difference between Medicare and Medicaid?

_____

_____

## ▶ VOCABULARY: Finish the Sentence

**Choose one of the following words or phrases to complete each sentence. Write the word or phrase on the correct line.**

hospitalization
specialist
surgeon
family practitioner
major medical

1. A _____ is a doctor who treats children and adults.

2. A _____ is a doctor who has studied a special area of medicine, such as skin diseases.

3. _____ is insurance that pays part of the cost of staying in the hospital.

4. _____ is insurance that pays for very large medical bills.

5. A _____ is a doctor who can operate.

 **THINKING AND WRITING** Think about the kind of health insurance you own. Is it enough protection for you? In your journal explain what your health insurance covers. Tell what you can do to improve your health insurance.

CHAPTER

SIX

# TAKING MEDICINE SAFELY

## Think About As You Read

▶ What kinds of illnesses do doctors treat with antibiotics?

▶ How do over-the-counter drugs differ from prescription drugs?

▶ How can you take medicine safely?

**Strep throat** is a sore throat caused by strep germs.

An **antibiotic** is medicine that can kill certain germs that cause illness.

Daniel Kent went to his doctor because he had a very sore throat. His doctor did a test that showed that Daniel had **strep throat**. The doctor told Daniel that he needed an **antibiotic** for ten days. After two days Daniel felt better, but he kept taking his medicine for ten days. When he returned to his doctor for another test, Daniel learned that he no longer had strep throat. Taking medicine correctly can help you have good health.

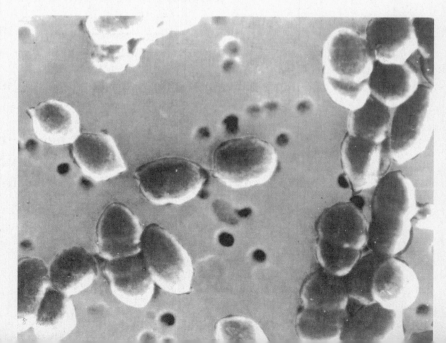

*A test can show if strep germs are causing a sore throat.*

56

## Understanding Antibiotics

**Viruses** and **bacteria** are two kinds of germs that can make you sick. Viruses cause the common cold, the flu, some sore throats, AIDS, and many other illnesses. Bacteria cause strep throat, scarlet fever, and many other diseases. Antibiotics are used to cure illnesses that are caused by bacteria. Antibiotics cannot cure illnesses caused by viruses.

You need a **prescription** from a doctor to buy an antibiotic. Different kinds of antibiotics are used for different kinds of bacteria. An expensive antibiotic may not be a better treatment than a cheaper one. Ask your doctor if you can use a **generic** antibiotic.

Follow your doctor's directions when taking an antibiotic. Find out if you need to take the medicine before or after meals. Take the antibiotic for all of the days that your doctor ordered. You can get sick again if you do not take the medicine for enough days. Flush left-over antibiotics down the toilet. Never share your antibiotics with others. Keep all medicines where children cannot reach them.

## Other Kinds of Medicine

Prescription drugs are used to treat many kinds of health problems. There are medicines to treat pain, **asthma**, high blood pressure, glaucoma, and many other problems. Ask your doctor about the correct way to take any prescription drug. You can save money by buying generic brands of many prescription drugs.

Each year people spend millions of dollars on **over-the-counter drugs**. You can buy these drugs without a prescription. Perhaps you have used over-the-counter drugs to treat headaches, colds, coughs, and other problems. These drugs do not cure illnesses. But they can help you feel better. You can save money by buying the store brands of headache, stomach, and cough medicines.

**Viruses** are germs that cause diseases. Antibiotics cannot kill viruses.

Some **bacteria** are germs that cause diseases. Antibiotics can kill bacteria.

A **prescription** is a written order from a doctor for a certain type of medicine.

A **generic** drug treats the same diseases and is made with the same ingredients as a drug from a well-known company. Generic drugs often cost less.

**Asthma** is a lung disease that makes it hard to breathe. People with asthma need to use prescription drugs correctly to control their disease.

**Over-the-counter drugs** are medicines that can be bought without a prescription.

A **dose** is the amount of medicine a person takes at one time.

**Side effects** are unpleasant and sometimes dangerous effects that medicines have on the body.

A **pharmacist** is a person who has a license to prepare prescription drugs.

Read the directions carefully on all over-the-counter drugs. Take the **dose** that is correct for you. The label will also tell you the doses that can be given to children of different ages. Many over-the-counter drugs should not be given to children who are less than two years old.

Medicines sometime cause **side effects**. Both prescription and over-the-counter drugs can cause side effects. For example, Daniel Kent's son got a stomachache from the antibiotic he took to cure an ear infection. The labels of over-the-counter drugs list all the side effects you may get. Call your doctor if you think you are having side effects from any type of medicine.

It can be dangerous to take an over-the-counter drug together with a prescription drug. It can also be dangerous to take more than one over-the-counter drug at a time. Check with your doctor or **pharmacist** before taking more than one medicine at a time.

## Compare Prescription Drugs and Over-the-Counter Drugs

**Prescription Drugs**

1. Buy with a prescription.

2. Visit a doctor to get a prescription.

3. Take the amount your doctor orders.

4. Buy prescription drugs at drugstores.

**All Medicine**

1. Take correct dose.

2. Follow directions.

3. Keep away from children.

4. Never take medicine and drink alcohol.

5. Store correctly.

**Over-the-Counter Drugs**

1. Buy without a prescription.

2. You do not need to see a doctor to get these.

3. Take only as much as you need for a few days.

4. Buy over-the-counter drugs in supermarkets, drugstores, and other stores.

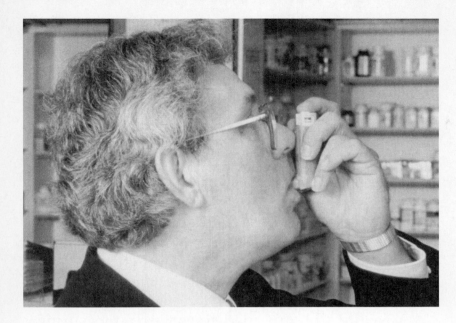

*To treat a health problem like asthma, you must use your medicine correctly.*

## Alcohol and Medicine

Alcohol changes the way medicine works in the body. It is dangerous to use alcohol and medicine together. For example, certain drugs are used to treat high blood pressure. When alcohol is used with this type of medicine, blood pressure can become very low. It can become so low that the person may die. To be safe, do not drink alcohol while you are using any kind of medicine.

## Using Medicine Safely

Heat, light, and air can damage medicine. It is important to store medicine correctly. Keep medicines in the containers they came in. Keep the containers closed tightly. Keep them in a cool, dark, dry place. Some medicines need to be kept in the refrigerator or they will spoil. Never store medicine near a stove.

The following rules can help you use medicine safely.

1. Do not take medicine in a dark room. You need to see what you are taking. Be sure you are taking the right medicine.

2. Read and follow directions for prescription drugs and for over-the-counter drugs. Do not take someone else's prescription drug.

3. Keep all medicine away from children. Keep medicine in a place that children cannot reach.

4. Take an over-the-counter drug only if you really need it.

5. Take the correct dose. Perhaps your doctor told you to take one pill three times a day. Do not take all three pills at once. Do not take two pills instead of three.

6. Measure all liquid medicines with a measuring spoon. Do not take more or less than the correct dose. Do not guess how much to take.

7. Stop taking any medicine that you think is causing side effects. Call your doctor at once and find out what you should do.

8. Check the **expiration date** on all over-the-counter drugs. Do not use a drug after its expiration date has passed.

Doctors now have more medicines to treat disease than ever before. Using medicine safely can help you protect your health.

The **expiration date** on a drug label is the last date that drug should be sold or used.

*Take the correct amount of medicine. Measure each dose carefully.*

**LIFE SKILLS Workshop**

## Reading Medicine Labels

### Reading a Prescription Medicine Label

The prescription label below is for an antibiotic. Read the label. Notice the following parts.

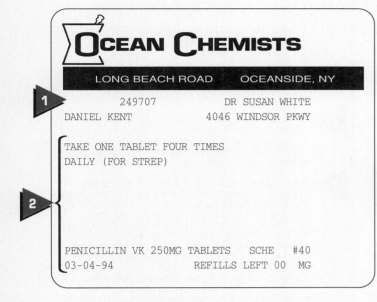

**OCEAN CHEMISTS**

LONG BEACH ROAD          OCEANSIDE, NY

**1** ▶   249707                DR SUSAN WHITE
DANIEL KENT          4046 WINDSOR PKWY

**2** ▶  TAKE ONE TABLET FOUR TIMES
DAILY (FOR STREP)

PENICILLIN VK 250MG TABLETS    SCHE    #40
03-04-94              REFILLS LEFT 00  MG

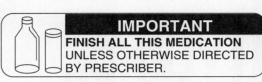

**IMPORTANT**
**FINISH ALL THIS MEDICATION** UNLESS OTHERWISE DIRECTED BY PRESCRIBER.    **3** ◀

TAKE MEDICATION ON AN EMPTY STOMACH 1 HOUR BEFORE OR 2 TO 3 HOURS AFTER A MEAL UNLESS OTHERWISE DIRECTED BY YOUR DOCTOR.

**1** ▶  This is the file number that the pharmacist gives your prescription. Use this number to get refills if needed.

**2** ▶  This part gives directions for taking the medicine correctly. It also tells what illness this medicine treats. It gives the name of the medicine. The doctor tells the pharmacist how many times this medicine can be refilled. Daniel cannot refill this prescription without seeing his doctor first.

**3** ▶  These warning labels are extra directions for taking this medicine correctly.

▼ ▼ ▼

**Use the prescription label to answer the following questions.**

**1.** What are the directions for taking this medicine? _____

_____

**2.** What is the name of this medicine? _____

**3.** What special directions are on the two warning labels?

_____

_____

**61**

# Reading an Over-the-Counter Drug Label

The label below is for Tylenol. Tylenol is made of a drug called **acetaminophen**. It is used instead of aspirin. Many people are allergic to aspirin. Aspirin can also upset your stomach. You can buy different brands of acetaminophen. Notice the following parts of the label.

**REGULAR STRENGTH**

# TYLENOL®

**Tablets**

**1** ▶ **Regular Strength TYLENOL® Tablets** act safely and quickly to provide temporary relief from: simple headache; minor muscular aches; the minor aches and pains associated with bursitis, neuralgia, sprains, overexertion, menstrual cramps; and from the discomfort of fever due to colds and 'flu'. Also for temporary relief of minor aches and pains of arthritis and rheumatism. (Caution: If pain persists for more than 10 days, or redness is present, or in arthritic or rheumatic conditions affecting children under 12 years, consult a physician immediately.)

**2** ▶ **How TYLENOL® acetaminophen products are different:**
- Contain no aspirin and are unlikely to cause the stomach upset or gastric irritation often associated with aspirin or aspirin-containing products.
- May be used safely and comfortably by most persons with peptic ulcer, when taken as directed for recommended conditions.

- Are not likely to cause a reaction in those who are allergic to aspirin, and are especially well suited for such persons.

**3** ▶ **DOSAGE:** Adults and children 12 years of Age and Older: 1 to 2 tablets 3 or 4 times daily. Children (6-12): 1/2 to 1 tablet 3 or 4 times daily. Consult a physician for use by children under 6. **INACTIVE INGREDIENTS:** Magnesium Stearate, Cellulose, Sodium Starch Glycolate, and Starch.

**4** ▶ **WARNING: DO NOT USE IF CARTON IS OPENED OR PRINTED RED NECK WRAP OR PRINTED FOIL INNER SEAL IS BROKEN.** DO NOT TAKE FOR PAIN FOR MORE THAN 10 DAYS (FOR ADULTS) OR 5 DAYS (FOR CHILDREN) AND DO NOT TAKE FOR FEVER FOR MORE THAN 3 DAYS UNLESS DIRECTED BY A PHYSICIAN. KEEP THIS AND ALL MEDICATION OUT OF THE REACH OF CHILDREN. AS WITH ANY DRUG, IF YOU ARE PREGNANT OR NURSING A BABY, SEEK THE ADVICE OF A HEALTH PROFESSIONAL BEFORE USING THIS PRODUCT. IN THE CASE OF ACCIDENTAL OVERDOSAGE, CONTACT A PHYSICIAN OR POISON CONTROL CENTER IMMEDIATELY.

See end panel for expiration date.
Store at room temperature.

**1** ▶ This tells what Tylenol does and when to call a doctor.

**2** ▶ This part explains how Tylenol is different from aspirin.

**3** ▶ The **dosage**, or the correct amount to take, is different for adults and children. The age of the child is also important.

**4** ▶ This warning tells how long you can safely take Tylenol.

▼ ▼ ▼

## Use the label to answer the following questions.

**1.** Name one kind of problem that you can take Tylenol for. _____

**2.** What is the dosage for an adult? _____

**3.** What is the dosage for a child 6–12 years of age? _____

**4.** What do you need to do for children under age 6? _____

**5.** How long can you safely take Tylenol if you have fever? _____

## ▶ WORKSHOP PRACTICE: Read a Medicine Label

Dr. Susan White gave Daniel Kent an antibiotic for his ear infection. Look at the label that the pharmacist put on Daniel's medicine. Answer the questions about this prescription drug.

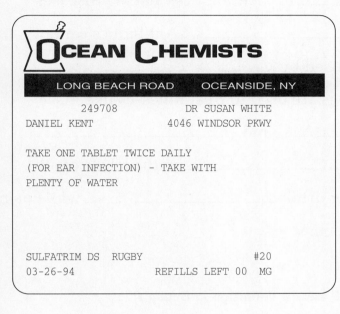

**OCEAN CHEMISTS**

LONG BEACH ROAD          OCEANSIDE, NY

249708                          DR SUSAN WHITE
DANIEL KENT                4046 WINDSOR PKWY

TAKE ONE TABLET TWICE DAILY
(FOR EAR INFECTION) - TAKE WITH
PLENTY OF WATER

SULFATRIM DS  RUGBY                    #20
03-26-94              REFILLS LEFT 00  MG

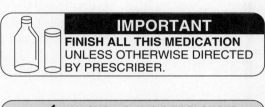

**IMPORTANT**
**FINISH ALL THIS MEDICATION**
UNLESS OTHERWISE DIRECTED
BY PRESCRIBER.

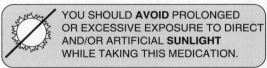

YOU SHOULD **AVOID** PROLONGED
OR EXCESSIVE EXPOSURE TO DIRECT
AND/OR ARTIFICIAL **SUNLIGHT**
WHILE TAKING THIS MEDICATION.

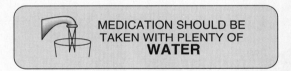

MEDICATION SHOULD BE
TAKEN WITH PLENTY OF
**WATER**

**1.** What are the directions for taking this medicine?

_____

_____

**2.** What is the name of this medicine? _____

**3.** Can Daniel have this prescription refilled? yes _____ no _____

**4.** The pharmacist put three warning labels with special directions on the pill bottle. What are the three special directions?

_____

_____

_____

_____

_____

COMPREHENSION: Finish the Paragraph

**Use the following words or phrases to finish the paragraph.**
**Write the words you choose on the correct lines.**

glaucoma
asthma
viruses
bacteria
alcohol
directions
antibiotic

You need a prescription from a doctor to buy an

_____ . Antibiotics can cure diseases

caused by _____ . Antibiotics cannot

cure illnesses caused by _____ .

Prescription drugs are used to treat illnesses like

_____ and _____ .

Follow the _____ on the labels of all

medicines. Never drink _____ while using

any kind of medicine.

 VOCABULARY: Matching

**Match the word or phrase in Group B with a definition in Group A.**
**Write the letter of the correct answer on the line.**

**Group A**

_____ 1. These are unpleasant effects that medicines
sometimes have on the body.

_____ 2. This is a written order from a doctor for a certain
medicine.

_____ 3. This person has a license to prepare prescription
drugs.

_____ 4. This is the last day a drug should be sold or used.

**Group B**

a. prescription

b. pharmacist

c. expiration date

d. side effects

 **THINKING AND WRITING** Think about the prescription and over-the-counter drugs you or your family have used in the last few months. In your journal explain why you took these medicines and how they affected you.

# HEALTH EMERGENCIES

## Think About As You Read

▶ When do you call EMS for help?

▶ What are the signs of a heart attack?

▶ What can you do to help someone who is choking or has stopped breathing?

Stacey Wong's father came to her home for dinner. At dinner he complained that he had sharp pains in his chest. He said it was hard for him to breathe. Stacey thought he might be having a heart attack. So she called **Emergency Medical Services (EMS)**. An EMS team came to Stacey's house and treated her father for a heart attack. They took him to the hospital for more treatment. By getting help quickly, Stacey saved her father's life.

**Emergency Medical Services (EMS)** are used to save people who are badly hurt or very sick.

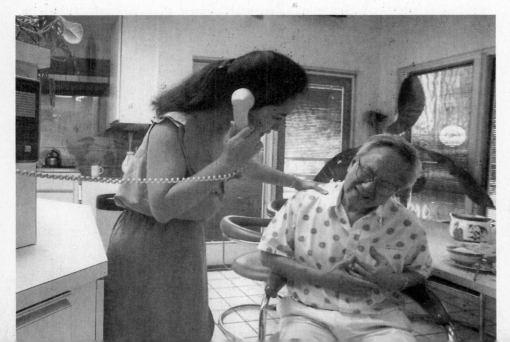

*Know the signs of a heart attack. Call EMS for help right away.*

**65**

## Getting Emergency Help

Always call EMS if you are faced with a health emergency. In many cities and towns, you dial 9–1–1 to call EMS. Find out the EMS phone number for your area. Place it near your phone. Remember to call EMS if a person stops breathing. Call EMS if a person has **severe bleeding**. Some other emergencies when you need EMS are heart attacks, choking, **shock**, and head injuries.

Perhaps you have taken a class in **first aid**. Then you have the training to handle an emergency. If you would like to learn first aid, call your local Red Cross to find out where and when you can take a class.

In an emergency, call EMS first. If you are with another person who can help, ask that person to call EMS. If you have first-aid training, you can start first aid right away.

## Rescue Breathing

Many problems can cause a person to stop breathing. A person may stop breathing because of a heart attack. Breathing can stop if a person used dangerous drugs or swallowed poison. Drinking too much alcohol or getting a bad electric shock can make a person stop breathing.

A person who chokes or stops breathing needs help quickly. Without help that person will die.

**Severe bleeding** is very heavy bleeding.

A person is in **shock** when the blood does not get enough food to the brain and other parts of the body.

**First aid** is the emergency care given to a hurt or sick person until that person can see a doctor.

*Take a first-aid class to learn how to handle health emergencies.*

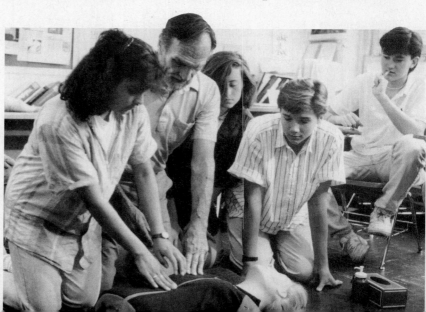

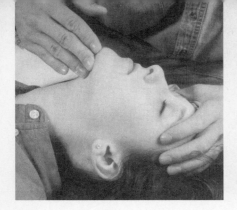

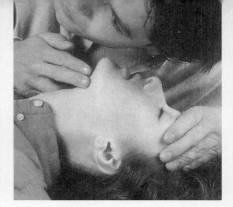

*Tilt the victim's head back to clear the airway.*

*Breathe into the victim's mouth until the chest rises.*

*Listen for air coming out. Repeat steps until help arrives or victim starts breathing.*

Always check to see if a sick or injured person has stopped breathing. Check the nose and mouth to see if anything is blocking air from moving in and out. If the chest stops moving up and down, you know that breathing has stopped.

Help the **victim** start breathing again by doing **rescue breathing**. Follow these steps.

1. Call EMS for help.

2. Lay the victim on his or her back. Do not put a pillow under the victim's head.

3. Put one of your hands under the victim's chin. Lift the chin. Put your other hand on the forehead. Tilt the head back. Close the nose with your fingers. Cover the victim's mouth with your mouth.

4. Breathe hard into the victim's mouth. Then listen for air going out. Repeat this every five seconds.

5. Do not stop rescue breathing until the victim starts breathing again or EMS arrives.

A **victim** is a person who is sick or hurt.

**Rescue breathing** is the way you breathe into the mouth of a person who has stopped breathing. Rescue breathing helps that person start breathing again.

## First Aid for Choking

One day you may be with someone who starts to choke. A person who is choking cannot breathe, talk, or cough. Choking people often grab at their throats. They need help fast.

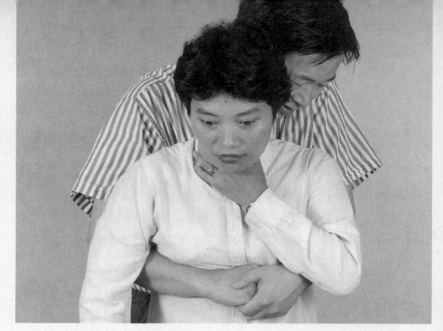

*Learn how to do abdominal thrusts to save a choking person.*

**Abdominal thrusts** can be used to save a person who is choking.

The **abdomen** is the part of your body that is below your chest and above your hips.

First, call EMS. Then do **abdominal thrusts** to save the victim.

1. Stand behind the choking person. Put your arms around the victim's waist.

2. Make a fist with one hand.

3. Put the thumb of your fist on the victim's **abdomen** below the ribs.

4. Push your fist into the abdomen with your other hand. Do quick, hard, upward pushes.

5. Keep making quick, hard pushes until the victim coughs out the object that caused choking. It is important for a doctor to check victims after they have stopped choking.

There are two ways you can save yourself if you start to choke while you are alone. Place the thumb of your fist against your abdomen. Then push your fist into your abdomen with your free hand. Do this until you cough up the object. You can also bend forward over the back of a chair. Quickly push your abdomen against the back of the chair. Do this again and again until you cough up the object.

# First Aid for Shock and Heart Attack

A person is in shock when the blood does not get enough food to the brain and other parts of the body. The heartbeat is very fast and blood pressure drops. Shock can cause death. Accident victims often go into shock. They need to be treated at once. Call EMS if you think someone is in shock.

Lay the shock victim flat on his or her back. Raise the victim's legs about ten inches. Cover the victim with a coat or blanket to keep the person warm. If the victim has stopped breathing, start rescue breathing.

These are the warning signs of a heart attack.

1. The victim has pain and pressure in the chest for two minutes or longer.

2. The victim finds it hard to breathe.

3. The heart beats very fast.

4. The victim has pain in the arms, neck, shoulders, or jaws.

5. The victim sweats a lot.

6. The victim feels dizzy and tired.

7. The victim has a sick feeling in the stomach or is throwing up.

A person who is having a heart attack may have only one or two of these signs. Call EMS right away if you think the victim may be having a heart attack. If there is time, call the victim's doctor, too. Then help the victim lie on his or her back to rest. Loosen the victim's clothing. Check that the victim does not stop breathing. If the victim stops breathing, start rescue breathing right away. Stay with the victim until EMS comes.

*When you cut yourself, stop the bleeding by raising the cut place above your heart.*

## First Aid for Wounds and Animal Bites

**Wounds** are cuts, bites, and scratches.

All **wounds** need first aid. Be careful when treating the wounds of others. Try not to let your skin touch the blood of other people. It is best to wear **latex** gloves when touching another person's blood. Use latex gloves once and throw them away. If you do not have latex gloves, use a thick cloth pad to treat the wound. Wash small wounds with soap and water. Cover them with a bandage.

**Latex** is a material like rubber.

People can die if they lose too much blood. So always try to stop severe bleeding. First, wash your hands and put on latex gloves. Then place a thick **sterile** pad or a clean cloth on the wound. Press hard to stop the bleeding. If the bleeding starts again, put another pad on top of the first one. Press hard on the wound again. Call EMS for help.

A **sterile** pad is free from germs and dirt.

Animal bites are also wounds. Wash the bite with warm water and soap. Cover it with a sterile pad. Call the police or animal control to have them find the animal. It is important to learn if the animal has **rabies**. If it has rabies, you will need rabies shots.

**Rabies** is a disease that can kill animals and people.

You can save a person who is sick or hurt by learning how to give the right emergency treatments. You can learn more about first aid at a course in your community. One day you may use first aid to help save another person.

# FIRST AID

| Injury | Symptoms | First Aid Treatment |
| --- | --- | --- |
| **Shock** | very fast pulse; blood pressure drops; victim may feel weak, thirsty, and/or confused | 1. Call EMS.<br>2. Help victim lie on his/her back with legs slightly raised.<br>3. Cover victim with a blanket. |
| **Fainting** | victim falls to ground and becomes unconscious | 1. Leave victim lying down.<br>2. Raise victim's legs slightly.<br>3. Check victim's breathing. Start rescue breathing if breathing has stopped.<br>4. Call EMS if victim does not wake up in a few minutes.<br>5. Get medical help when victim wakes up. |
| **Breathing stops** | no air comes out of nose or mouth, chest stops moving, lips and fingernails turn blue, victim becomes unconscious, no pulse | 1. Call EMS.<br>2. Do rescue breathing until breathing starts again or EMS arrives. |
| **Heart attack** | pain in chest; possible pain in arms, neck, and/or jaw; difficulty breathing; shortness of breath; dizzy; sweating; lips and skin may turn blue; indigestion; victim becomes unconscious | 1. Call EMS at once.<br>2. Person trained in CPR can begin doing CPR if heart stops beating.<br>3. Call victim's doctor if there is time.<br>4. Keep victim warm and comfortable.<br>5. Start rescue breathing if victim stops breathing. |
| **Nosebleed** | blood flows from nose | 1. Have victim sit up and lean forward.<br>2. Press both nostrils of victim together. Have victim breathe through mouth for 10–15 minutes.<br>3. Call a doctor if bleeding does not stop after 10–15 minutes. |
| **Heatstroke** | skin is very red and hot, no sweating, body temperature rises fast, victim feels weak, pulse is fast and weak, victim may feel faint or become unconscious | 1. Undress victim.<br>2. Place victim in the shade or a cool place if possible.<br>3. Place victim in a tub of cool water or wrap a cold, wet towel around victim.<br>4. Call EMS. |
| **Broken bone** | pain and swelling around the injury; victim cannot use the injured hand, arm, leg, or foot | 1. Call EMS if needed.<br>2. Treat for shock if needed.<br>3. If it is a bad break, avoid moving person until help arrives. If victim must be moved, place injured arm or leg in a splint. Tie splint to arm or leg at points above and below the injury.<br>4. Have victim see doctor. |
| **Eye injury** | pain and redness in eye | 1. Wash victim's eye with clean water for 10–20 minutes. Pour water from inner corner of eye toward outer corner.<br>2. Cover eye with sterile pad.<br>3. Have victim see eye doctor. |
| **Severe bleeding** | bleeding does not stop | 1. Wash wound with soap and water.<br>2. Cover wound with thick sterile pad.<br>3. Press hard on wound to stop the bleeding.<br>4. Call EMS. |

**Note:** Cut out this chart and tape it to a bathroom wall or medicine chest. Use it to know what to do in an emergency.

## LIFE SKILLS Workshop

# Completing a Hospital Emergency Room Form

Stacey Wong visited a hospital emergency room after she was bitten by a dog one night. She completed the emergency room form on page 73. Notice the following parts.

**1** ▶ **Information About the Patient.** This part asks information about the patient. Stacey's race is Asian. Race can be Anglo, African, Hispanic, or Native American.

**2** ▶ **Next of Kin.** Your next of kin is a family member who can be called. Some emergency room forms ask for a contact person. The contact person can be a close friend, neighbor, or family member.

**3** ▶ **Insurance Information.** Stacey's policy number is the number she was given by her insurance company. The prefix group number is the numbers or letters that are written before the policy number. The suffix group number is the letters or numbers that are written after the policy number.

**4** ▶ **Allergies to Medication.** It is important to write the names of medicines that give you allergies. Then the hospital doctor will not give you these medicines.

**5** ▶ **Your Injury or Illness.** Stacey wrote why she came to the hospital emergency room. She also wrote when her accident happened and what medicine she took. It is important to write the names of medicines that you are taking.

▼ ▼ ▼

**Use Stacey's form to answer the following questions.**

**1.** Who is Stacey's next of kin? _____

**2.** What is the name of Stacey's health insurance company?

_____

**3.** What happens when Stacey takes aspirin?

_____

**4.** What medicine did Stacey take for pain?

_____

# EMERGENCY MEDICAL SERVICES SIGN-IN SHEET

**1**

PATIENT NAME:

LAST: _Wong_     FIRST: _Stacey_     BIRTHDATE: _12/19/66_

STREET ADDRESS: _902 E. 9th St._     CITY: _Los Angeles_ STATE: _CA_ ZIP: _90015_

TELEPHONE #_(213)555-6868_ MARITAL STATUS: Married  Divorced  Separated  (Single)  Widowed

RACE: _Asian_  RELIGION: _Catholic_ PATIENT SOCIAL SECURITY NO. _233-22-8774_

FAMILY DOCTOR: _Alice Strong_
 (Full Name)

**2**

NEXT OF KIN (Name): _Sue Wong_     RELATIONSHIP: _mother_

ADDRESS: _3230 Franklin Ave._     PHONE: _213-555-7515_

**3**

NAME OF INS. CO. _American Health Insurance_

POLICY #: _233-22-8774_     PREFIX GROUP # _47454 RA_ SUFFIX: _SH_

ADDRESS FOR INS. OTHER THAN MEDICARE: _1600 Ash Blvd., Sacramento, CA_

RETIRED: YES_____  NO _✓_  IF YES, FROM WHERE:_____

NAME OF POLICY HOLDER: _Stacey Wong_     EMPLOYER: _24-Hour Mart_

OCCUPATION: _salesclerk_     ADDRESS: _3470 W. 6th St._

PHONE #_(213) 555-6870_

**4**

ANY ALLERGIES TO MEDICATION? _yes_

IF YES, EXPLAIN _Aspirin gives me a rash._

DESCRIBE YOUR INJURY, ILLNESS: _I was bitten on my right leg by a stray dog. My leg has been bleeding._

**5**

WHEN DID YOUR ILLNESS OR INJURY OCCUR: (DATE & TIME) _Feb. 24 at 10:30 at night_

DO YOU TAKE MEDICATION? (LIST THEM) _I took two regular acetaminophen pills for the pain in my leg._

▶ **WORKSHOP PRACTICE: Complete an Emergency Room Form**

One day you may need treatment at a hospital emergency room. You may have to complete a hospital emergency room form. Complete the sample form on this page. Use the information on pages 72–73 as a guide.

### EMERGENCY MEDICAL SERVICES SIGN-IN SHEET

PATIENT NAME:

LAST:_____ FIRST:_____ BIRTHDATE:_____

STREET ADDRESS:_____ CITY:_____ STATE:____ ZIP:_____

TELEPHONE #_____ MARITAL STATUS: Married  Divorced  Separated  Single  Widowed

RACE:_____ RELIGION:_____PATIENT SOCIAL SECURITY NO._____

FAMILY DOCTOR:_____
          (Full Name)

NEXT OF KIN (Name):_____ RELATIONSHIP:_____

ADDRESS:_____ PHONE: _____

NAME OF INS. CO._____

POLICY #:_____ PREFIX GROUP #_____ SUFFIX:_____

ADDRESS FOR INS. OTHER THAN MEDICARE:_____

RETIRED: YES_____  NO_____ IF YES, FROM WHERE:_____

NAME OF POLICY HOLDER:_____ EMPLOYER:_____

OCCUPATION:_____ ADDRESS:_____

                                 PHONE #_____

ANY ALLERGIES TO MEDICATION?_____

IF YES, EXPLAIN_____

DO YOU TAKE MEDICATION? (LIST THEM)_____

_____

▶ **COMPREHENSION: Circle the Answer**
**Draw a circle around the correct answer.**

**1.** Which problems do <u>not</u> need help from EMS?

    heart attack or severe bleeding

    common cold and ear infection

    choking and head injury

**2.** What can you do to help a person who has stopped breathing?

    do rescue breathing

    do abdominal thrusts

    cover person with a blanket

**3.** Which is <u>not</u> a sign of a heart attack?

    pain in the chest    sick feeling in the stomach    sore throat

**4.** What disease can you get if you are bitten by an animal?

    chicken pox    rabies    flu

**5.** What do you need to wear if you have to touch another person's blood?

    cotton gloves    wool gloves    latex gloves

## VOCABULARY: Writing with Vocabulary Words
**Use six or more of the following words or phrases to write
a paragraph about handling health emergencies.**

first aid        _____
severe bleeding  _____
EMS            _____
wounds         _____
shock          _____
victim         _____
rescue breathing  _____
abdominal thrusts  _____
sterile        _____
abdomen       _____

                 _____

**THINKING AND WRITING** Imagine you are with a person who is in shock and has stopped breathing. The victim is not able to talk to you. What would you do to help this victim? In your journal tell what you would do to save this victim's life.

# PREVENTING ACCIDENTS

## Think About As You Read

▶ Why do drivers need to avoid using alcohol and certain kinds of medicine when driving?

▶ How can you prevent poisoning in your home?

▶ How can you prevent kitchen and bathroom accidents?

**B**ike riding is one of Lisa Green's favorite sports. She is a careful rider who always wears a helmet. Her bike has good brakes and enough air in both tires. Lisa wears light-colored clothes when she rides so that drivers can see her easily. To avoid accidents, Lisa obeys all traffic rules.

Each year many people are hurt and killed in accidents. By learning good safety habits, you can prevent many kinds of accidents.

*Good safety habits prevent injuries. Wear a helmet when you ride a bike.*

*Be sure you have the correct amount of air in your tires.*

## Safety for Bike Riders and Drivers

You may ride a bike to travel to work or to school. You can also make bike riding a sport that you enjoy. To ride safely, ride a bike that is the right size for you. Both children and adults need helmets whenever they ride. Use hand signals when you make turns or stops. It is dangerous to wear headphones when riding a bike.

Safety is also important when driving a car. It is against the law to drink alcohol and drive a car. More than half of all car accidents are caused by drivers who have been drinking alcohol. Even a small amount of alcohol can make it easier for you to get into an accident.

It is dangerous to drive when taking any medicine that can cause **drowsiness**. Check with your doctor or pharmacist to learn if your prescription medicines can make you sleepy. Check the warning labels on all over-the-counter drugs. Sometimes the label will tell you not to drive because a certain medicine causes drowsiness.

**Drowsiness** means feeling sleepy.

Be sure your car has been checked for safety. Your car needs good brakes and tires. If you are buying a car, try to buy one that has air bags. All passengers need to wear seat belts at all times.

Small children need to ride in special safety seats in cars. A seat belt alone cannot protect a small child. Small babies need a different kind of seat than a child who can sit and walk. Use the right kind of seats for the children who ride in your car. To be safe, these seats need to be used correctly. So follow the directions that come with car seats for children.

## Preventing Falls and Poisoning

Many people are hurt each year because they fall in their own homes. To prevent falls, wear shoes and not just socks when walking around your home. It is easy to slip on floors that have too much wax. So avoid using too much wax. Wipe all spills from the floor as soon as they happen. Do not leave objects on the floor or steps that people can trip on. Put rubber mats under small loose rugs so they do not move when you walk on them.

Many of the cleaning products, medicines, and beauty products in your home are **poisonous**. Check the warning labels on your **detergent**, paints, nail polish remover, and hair spray. All of these products are poisonous, too. Products like paint and hair spray are poisonous if swallowed. Some products can harm you if you breathe in their **fumes**.

A **poisonous** product contains poison and can be very harmful to you if taken into your body the wrong way.

**Detergent** is soap that can be used for cleaning clothes, dishes, floors, and other parts of a home.

**Fumes** are the gases given off by products like paint and nail polish.

*Make sure children are buckled up in car seats.*

Follow these rules to prevent poisoning.

1. Store all medicines, make-up, cleaning products, and beauty products on a high shelf that children cannot reach. If possible, keep these supplies in a locked closet.

2. Never put poisonous products like detergent in food containers. Keep poisonous products in the containers they came in. Leave the warning labels on the containers.

3. Teach children not to eat house plants. Many house plants are poisonous.

4. Keep the windows open when using paints, paint thinners, and other products that give off fumes.

Poisons can kill people fast. Get help quickly if you believe a person swallowed a poison. Call your Poison Control Center. Keep the phone number of your Poison Control Center by your phone near the EMS number. Tell the person at the center which poison was swallowed. The person at the center will tell you what to do. Sometimes the poison victim is **unconscious**. Then you may not know what kind of poison was swallowed. Call EMS for help at once. Call EMS if someone becomes sick from breathing poisonous fumes.

People are **unconscious** when they have passed out and cannot feel things or move.

**CAUTION:**
Avoid contact with eyes, skin, and mucous membranes. Do not mix with acids or other household chemicals. In case of eye contact, flush thoroughly with water. If swallowed, give one or two glasses of water or milk. Call physician. Use only in well ventilated areas. Do not use on fabrics or surfaces which may be discolored or damaged. Rinse immediately upon contact with porcelain tu
KEEP OUT OF REACH OF CHILDREN.

CAUTION: If swallowed, give a glassful of water or milk. Call a physician. In case of eye contact, flush with water. KEEP OUT OF REACH OF CHILDREN.

WARNING:
Precautionary Statements
Hazards to humans and domestic animals.
Causes substantial but temporary eye injury. Do not get in eyes or on clothing. Harmful if swallowed. May irritate skin. For prolonged use, wear gloves.
**Practical treatment.** If in eyes, remove contact lenses and rinse with plenty of water for 15 minutes. If swallowed, drink a glassful of water. Call physician in either case. If in contact with skin, immediately remove contamin... with and wash skin thorough...

*Read and follow the warning labels on household products.*

## Preventing Kitchen and Bathroom Accidents

Most home accidents happen in the kitchen and bathroom. These safety rules can help you avoid accidents.

1. If you have young children in your home, put child-proof locks on all kitchen and bathroom cabinets.

2. Do not leave young children alone in the kitchen or bathroom.

3. Never hang kitchen towels above the stove to dry.

4. In the bathroom use plastic cups and bottles that cannot break.

5. Dry your hands before using hair dryers and other electric **appliances**.

6. Do not stand in a puddle of water when using an electric appliance. You can get an electric shock.

7. Use a rubber bath mat in your tub and shower to prevent falls.

8. Never use an electric heater in your bathroom or near your kitchen sink. You may get an electric shock.

**Appliances** are machines like hair dryers that help you do certain jobs.

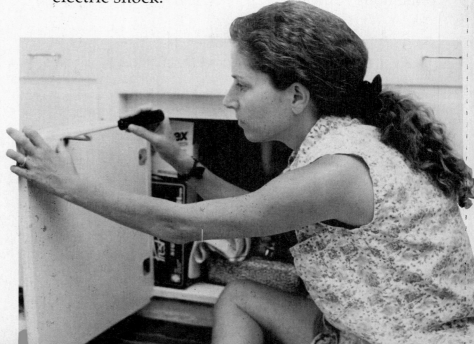

*To child-proof your home, put child-proof locks on cabinets.*

## Preventing Other Home Accidents

Many home fires are caused by burning cigarettes. Dangerous fires can start when people smoke cigarettes in bed. Never allow anyone in your home to smoke in bed.

Your home needs a **smoke detector** that works. Check the batteries once a month. Your smoke detector will warn you if a fire is starting.

Guns are dangerous weapons to have in a home. If you own a gun, always keep it in a locked closet. Keep bullets in a separate locked closet.

Electricity can be dangerous if it is not used carefully. Cover electric outlets with safety covers to prevent children from playing with them. Sometimes the **fuse** in your home will blow if you use too many appliances at once. Always replace a blown fuse with another fuse that is the same size.

The chart on this page shows other ways to use electricity safely.

Take a walk through your home and see where accidents can happen. Make those parts of your home safer. Learning how to prevent accidents will help you have good health and enjoy life.

A **smoke detector** is a small alarm that buzzes when smoke is in a room.

A **fuse** is a safety wire that melts and shuts off the electricity when too much electricity is used at one time.

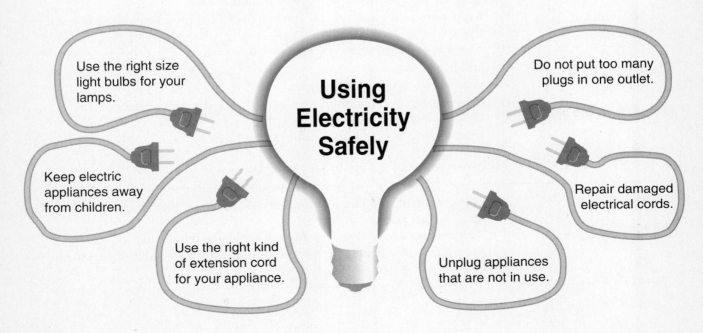

Use the right size light bulbs for your lamps.

Do not put too many plugs in one outlet.

Keep electric appliances away from children.

**Using Electricity Safely**

Repair damaged electrical cords.

Use the right kind of extension cord for your appliance.

Unplug appliances that are not in use.

# HOME SAFETY

| Problem | How to Be Safe |
|---------|----------------|
| **Being safe at home** | 1. Never open the door for a person without first checking to find out who wants to come in.<br>2. Never allow strangers to come into your home.<br>3. Call 9-1-1 or the operator if there is an emergency.<br>4. Use good locks on your front and back doors.<br>5. Lock all doors and windows when you leave your home.<br>6. Keep your EMS number and your Poison Control Center number near your phone. |
| **Poisons** | 1. Buy medicines and cleansers in childproof containers.<br>2. Check expiration dates on all medicines. Flush old medicine down the toilet. Check with your pharmacist if you have questions.<br>3. Keep all poisons, chemicals, and medicines in places children cannot reach.<br>4. Keep chemicals, cleansers, and medicines in the containers they were packed.<br>5. Call the Poison Control Center or EMS before you try to help someone who has swallowed a poison. |
| **Food poisoning** | 1. Never eat food from rusted, leaking, or swollen cans.<br>2. Check expiration dates on food. Do not eat food that is older than the expiration date.<br>3. Wash tops of cans before opening them.<br>4. Do not eat raw meat, chicken, fish, or eggs. |
| **Kitchen accidents** | 1. Do not leave small children alone in the kitchen.<br>2. Never allow children to play with plastic bags.<br>3. Do not wear long, loose sleeves when cooking. They can catch on fire.<br>4. Keep rags, paper, and towels away from the stove.<br>5. Keep a fire extinguisher in the kitchen to put out fires. Know how to use it to put out fires. |
| **Accidents in the bathroom** | 1. Use plastic cups and bottles.<br>2. Wipe all spills from the floor.<br>3. Never leave small children alone in the bathroom. Never leave small children alone in the bathtub.<br>4. Do not leave medicine in a medicine chest that small children can reach or open.<br>5. Never use electrical appliances in or near water. |
| **Storage areas** | 1. Do not keep old clothes, newspapers, and furniture that people no longer use.<br>2. Keep storage areas locked so children cannot go into them.<br>3. Keep flammable liquids in their containers. Keep flammable liquids away from heat or fire. |

## Reading Warning Labels

All over-the-counter drugs come with warnings on their labels. The warning label below is for the over-the-counter drug Benadryl. People with colds and allergies take this drug to feel better. Notice the warnings on the label.

**WARNINGS:** Do not take this product if you have asthma, glaucoma, emphysema, chronic pulmonary disease, shortness of breath, difficulty in breathing or difficulty in urination due to enlargement of the prostate gland unless directed by a physician. May cause excitability especially in children. May cause marked drowsiness; alcohol, sedatives, and tranquilizers may increase the drowsiness effect. Avoid driving a motor vehicle or operating machinery or drinking alcoholic beverages. Do not take this product if you are taking sedatives or tranquilizers without first consulting your doctor. Do not use any other products containing diphenhydramine while using this product. As with any drug, if you are pregnant or nursing a baby, seek the advice of a health professional before using this product. **KEEP THIS AND ALL DRUGS OUT OF THE REACH OF CHILDREN.** In case of accidental overdose, seek professional assistance or contact a Poison Control Center immediately.

▼ ▼ ▼

**Answer these questions about the warning label on Benadryl.**

**1.** Who should not take Benadryl?

_____

_____

**2.** What side effects can the drug cause?

_____

_____

**3.** What do you need to avoid doing when taking Benadryl?

_____

_____

**4.** What do you need to do if you take an overdose?

_____

_____

**83**

▶ **WORKSHOP PRACTICE: Read a Warning Label**

The Life Skills Workshop showed you how to read warning labels on medicines. It is also important for you to read the warning labels on other products in your home. Read the warning label from a can of paint. Then answer the questions.

---

**CAUTION:** MAY CAUSE EYE AND SKIN IRRITATION ON CONTACT. INHALATION OF SPRAY MIST MAY CAUSE RESPIRATORY TRACT IRRITATION. MAY BE HARMFUL IF SWALLOWED.

**FIRST AID:** In case of skin contact, wash off quickly with soap and water. For eye contact, flush immediately with large amounts of water, especially under lids. Always paint with adequate ventilation. If inhalation causes irritation or other discomfort, move to fresh air. If discomfort or irritation persists, seek medical attention.

**IMPORTANT!** Spray mist contains particles that may cause irritation of respiratory tract if inhaled. If this paint is spray applied, the use of a respirator is recommended. Obtain professional advice for proper selection, fit, and use of respirator. If sanding of any paint is done, wear a dust mask.

**For emergency information call (800) 545-2643.**
**For additional information, refer to the Material Safety Data Sheet for this product.**

**KEEP OUT OF REACH OF CHILDREN.**

---

**1.** How can paint be harmful? _____

_____

**2.** What should you do if paint gets in your eyes? _____

_____

**3.** If you have trouble breathing, what do you need to do?

_____

_____

▶ **VOCABULARY: Find the Meaning**
**On the line write the word or phrase that best completes each sentence.**

**1.** Medicine that makes you sleepy causes _____ .

drowsiness      happiness      high blood pressure

**2.** A person who has passed out and cannot feel things or move is

_____ .

awake        unconscious        dreaming

**3.** Soaps that are used for cleaning dishes, clothes, floors, and other parts

of the home are _____ .

deodorants        detergents        wax

**4.** The gases given off by products like paint and nail polish remover are

_____ .

fuses        nutrients        fumes

**5.** A _____ is a safety wire that melts and shuts off the
power when too much electricity is used at one time.

fuse        appliance        fume

► **COMPREHENSION: True or False**
**Write True next to each sentence that is true. Write False next to
each sentence that is false. There are two false sentences.**

_____ **1.** It is against the law to drink alcohol and drive a car.

_____ **2.** Passengers always need to wear seat belts in cars.

_____ **3.** It is safe to wear headphones when riding a bike.

_____ **4.** Call EMS if you do not know what kind of poison
a person swallowed.

_____ **5.** Close your windows when using paint and paint thinners.

**On the lines that follow, rewrite the two false sentences to make them true.**

_____

_____

 **THINKING AND WRITING** What areas of your home could be made safer? What could
you change to improve the safety in your home? Explain in
your journal how you can make your home safer.

**85**

# CROSSWORD PUZZLE: Safety First

Use the clues below to complete the crossword puzzle on page 87.
Choose from the words listed on page 87.
For an extra challenge, cover up the words.

**Across**

3. A ------ is a doctor who treats children.

5. A ------ is a safety wire that melts and shuts off the electricity when too much electricity is used at one time.

6. A germ that causes a disease and cannot be killed by antibiotics is a

   ------ .

8. The ------ is the part of your body that is below your chest and above your hips.

9. A ------ pad is free from germs and dirt.

10. A government health insurance program to provide health care for people with low incomes is ------ .

**Down**

1. Germs that cause diseases and that can be killed by antibiotics are

   ------ .

2. A ------ is a person who is sick or hurt.

3. A ------ is a written order from a doctor for a certain type of medicine.

4. ------ means feeling sleepy.

5. The emergency care given to a hurt or sick person until that person can see a doctor is ------ .

7. An ------ is medicine that can kill certain bacteria that cause illness.

abdomen            first aid            prescription

antibiotic         fuse                 sterile

bacteria           Medicaid             victim

drowsiness         pediatrician         virus

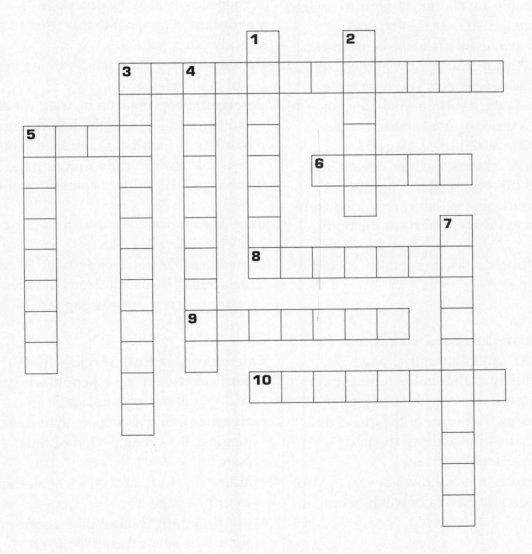

# Glossary

## A

**abdomen** The part of the body that is below the chest and above the hips. page 68

**abdominal thrusts** Movements that can be used to save a person who is choking. page 68

**acetaminophen** A substitute for aspirin. Many people are allergic to aspirin. page 62

**aerobic exercise** An exercise that uses repeated activity to make the heart work faster and make you breathe harder. page 27

**allergies** Bad side effects you may have when you take a certain medicine. page 40

**antibiotic** Medicine that can kill certain germs that cause illness. page 56

**appliances** Machines like hair dryers that help you do certain jobs. page 80

**arteries** Blood vessels that carry blood from the heart to different parts of the body. page 27

**asthma** A lung disease that makes it hard to breathe. page 57

## B

**bacteria** Germs that cause diseases. Antibiotics can kill bacteria. page 57

**bladder** The organ that holds liquid waste, or urine, until it leaves the body. page 38

**blood pressure** The force of the blood as it moves against the walls of the body's blood vessels. page 15

**bowel** The intestine. Solid waste leaves your body when you have a bowel movement. page 38

## C

**calories** The way energy we get from food is measured. page 15

**cancer** A disease in which unhealthy cells attack and destroy the body's normal cells. page 7

**cholesterol** A fatty substance in the blood. High amounts can cause heart disease. page 15

## D

**deep-breathing exercise** An exercise in which you take a deep breath, hold it, and then slowly breathe out. page 31

**deodorant** A product that is used to stop body odor. page 8

**dependent** A person whose living expenses are paid by an adult. page 52

**detergent** Soap that can be used for cleaning clothes and items in the home. page 78

**disability** A problem that makes a person less able to do certain things. page 28

**discharge** A liquid that comes out of the body. page 38

**dose** The amount of medicine a person takes at one time. page 58

**drowsiness** Feeling sleepy. page 77

**drug abuse** The use of drugs in ways that are not correct or safe. page 9

## E

**Emergency Medical Services (EMS)** Services used to save people who are badly hurt or very sick. page 65

**endurance** Being able to do activities, like jogging, for a long period of time. page 29

**examine** To study and check something carefully. page 39

**expiration date** The last date a product should be sold or used. page 60

## F

**family practitioner** A doctor who is trained to treat both children and adults. page 49

**fiber** A carbohydrate from plants that helps the body remove wastes. page 17

**first aid** The emergency care given to a hurt or sick person. page 66

**floss** To clean between your teeth with a strong thread called dental floss. page 6

**fumes** The gases given off by products like paint and nail polish. page 78

**fuse** A safety wire that melts and shuts off the electricity when too much electricity is used at one time. page 81

## G

**generic drug** A drug with no company name. A generic drug treats the same diseases and is made with the same ingredients as a drug from a well-known company. page 57

**glaucoma** An eye disease in which pressure inside the eye can cause blindness. page 36

## H

**habits** Behaviors that people do often. page 5

**health insurance** Insurance that helps you pay for different types of health care. page 48

**Health Maintenance Organization (HMO)** A group of doctors and hospitals that have agreed to provide medical services at a special rate to their members. page 51

**hospitalization insurance** Insurance that pays part of the cost of staying in a hospital. page 50

**hygiene** The way you keep your body clean and healthy. page 8

## I

**illegal** Against the law. page 9

**ingredients** Foods that are used to make a product. page 22

**internist** A doctor who treats diseases and problems found in adults. page 49

## L

**latex** A material like rubber. page 70

## M

**major medical insurance** Insurance that pays for very large medical bills, such as surgery. page 50

**Medicaid** A government health insurance program to provide health care for people with low incomes. page 51

**Medicare** A government health insurance program that pays for hospital stays for people who are at least 65 years old. page 51

**mole** A black or brown spot on the skin. page 8

## N

**next of kin** A person related to you by blood or marriage. page 72

**nutrients** Substances in food that the body needs for health and life. The six nutrients are carbohydrates, proteins, fats, vitamins, minerals, and water. page 15

## O

**osteoporosis** A disease in which the bones lose the mineral called calcium and become weaker. page 27

**overdose** Taking too much of a medicine. page 83

**over-the-counter drugs** Medicines that can be bought without a prescription. page 57

**overweight** Weighing more than the correct weight for age, height, and body frame. page 14

## P

**pasta** Foods like macaroni, spaghetti, and noodles. page 21

**pediatrician** A doctor who treats children. page 49

**pharmacist** A person who has a license to prepare prescription drugs. page 58

**poisonous** Products that can be very harmful to you. page 78

**posture** The way you carry your body when you sit and stand. page 7

**poultry** Birds such as chickens, turkeys, and ducks that are used for food. page 21

**prescription** A written order from a doctor for a certain type of medicine. page 57

**R**

**rabies** A disease that can kill animals and people. page 70

**rescue breathing** The way you breathe into the mouth of a person who has stopped breathing. It helps that person start breathing again. page 67

**S**

**severe bleeding** Very heavy bleeding. page 66

**shock** A state or condition when the blood does not get enough food to the brain and other parts of the body. page 66

**side effects** Unpleasant and sometimes dangerous effects that medicines can have on the body. page 58

**smoke detector** A small alarm that buzzes when smoke is in a room. page 81

**sodium** A mineral found in salt. page 22

**specialist** A doctor who has studied a special area of medicine. page 49

**sterile** Free from germs and dirt. page 70

**strep throat** A sore throat caused by strep germs. page 56

**stress** The way the body responds to emotional, physical, and social pressures. page 27

**sunscreen lotion** Blocks the sun's harmful rays from damaging your skin. page 7

**surgeon** A doctor who can operate, or do surgery. page 48

**surgery** The use of medical tools to operate on the body. page 50

**T**

**testes** Male sex organs. page 39

**tooth decay** When acids in the mouth make a small hole on the surface of a tooth. page 17

**tumor** A lump that can grow anywhere in the body. A tumor can be made of normal cells or cancer cells. page 38

**U**

**unconscious** When someone has passed out or fainted. page 79

**U.S. Recommended Daily Allowances (U.S. RDA)** The amounts of nutrients you need each day. page 22

**V**

**vaccines** Medicines that protect you from getting certain diseases. page 36

**victim** A person who is sick or hurt. page 67

**virus** A germ that causes diseases. Antibiotics cannot kill a virus. page 57

**W**

**wart** A small lump on the skin that is caused by a virus. page 38

**weight-bearing exercise** Exercise that makes you push against weight to make your bones and muscles stronger. page 28

**workout** A group of exercises that helps make the heart and the muscles stronger. page 29

**wounds** Cuts, bites, and scratches. page 70

# Answer Key

## Chapter 1

### Page 11 Workshop

**1.** for a complete checkup

**2.** Friday, April 22, at 4:30 P.M.

**3.** her insurance card and shot record

**4.** call at least one day before

### Page 12 Workshop Practice

**1.** I would like to make an appointment with Dr. Sinclair for May 5 at 4:30.

**2.** Answers will vary.

**3.** Answers will vary.

### Pages 12–13 Vocabulary

**1.** cancer

**2.** illegal

**3.** mole

**4.** drug abuse

**5.** deodorant

### Page 13 Comprehension

Habits that help you stay well are <u>good health habits</u>. Three examples of good health habits are <u>practicing good posture</u>, <u>controlling your weight</u>, and <u>washing your hands</u> before eating. A good habit that helps you protect your skin from the sun is using <u>sunscreen lotion</u>. Avoid bad health habits like <u>smoking cigarettes</u>, <u>abusing drugs</u>, and <u>drinking alcohol</u>.

## Chapter 2

### Page 22 Workshop

**1.** 1

**2.** 120

**3.** 2 g

**4.** 10 g

**5.** 170 mg

**6.** wheat flour

**7.** potato chips

### Page 24 Workshop Practice

**1.** pretzels

**2.** potato chips

**3.** pretzels

**4.** pretzels

**5.** Answers will vary.

### Pages 24–25 Comprehension

**1.** The six nutrients that come from food are carbohydrates, proteins, fats, vitamins, minerals, and water.

**2.** The four types of foods to avoid and examples of each kind of food are salty foods (salty chips, salty nuts, canned soups, smoked meat and fish, lunch meats); foods high in cholesterol (egg yolks, red meat, liver, and butter); fatty foods (whole milk, cream, chips, bacon, fried chicken, and hot dogs); and sugar (candy, cakes, cookies, soda, and cereals that are high in sugar).

**3.** The body uses more calories when people exercise. The body uses its own fat for energy and people lose weight.

**4.** Bread, cereal, pasta, and other grains supply most of the calories in a healthy diet.

**5.** Fruits, vegetables, and whole grains are less expensive than meat, fish, and poultry. Fresh fruits and vegetables in season are cheaper. Cereals with little or no sugar are less expensive. Powdered milk is cheaper than fresh milk.

### Page 25 Vocabulary

**1.** d

**2.** e

**3.** a

**4.** c

**5.** b

## Chapter 3

### Page 32 Workshop

**1.** Any of the following are correct: rolling head from side to side, touching toes, stretching arms above the head and to the sides, rolling the shoulders forward and backward, swinging arms from side to side, bending the knees up and down, bending at the waist from side to side

2. jogging in place and jumping rope or jumping rope and riding an exercise bike

3. fast walking, jogging, bicycle riding, swimming, or skating

4. repeat warm-up exercises slowly or walk slowly for 10 minutes

## Page 33 Workshop Practice

Exercise programs will vary.

## Pages 33–34 Comprehension

1. True

2. False; Jogging is a good aerobic exercise.

3. True

4. True

5. False; You should exercise at least three times a week to make your heart stronger.

## Page 34 Vocabulary

1. Stress

2. endurance

3. osteoporosis

4. arteries

5. Aerobic exercise

## Chapter 4

### Pages 40–43 Workshop

1. asthma

2. Vanceril inhaler, Proventil inhaler

3. penicillin

4. not earning enough money; worrying about his father who had a heart attack

5. coughing for days after an asthma attack

6. flu

7. 1984 for an appendectomy

8. high blood pressure, heart attack, glaucoma, arthritis, asthma

9. developing a good diet and exercise program; ways to help him manage his asthma better

## Page 44 Workshop Practice

The answers on the form will vary. Print clearly and fill out the form completely.

## Pages 44–45 Comprehension

1. every year

2. once a month

3. when cancer cells have spread throughout the body

4. two weeks

5. rest and drink liquids

## Page 45 Vocabulary

Answers will vary. You may use more than one vocabulary word in a sentence.

## Page 47 Crossword Puzzle

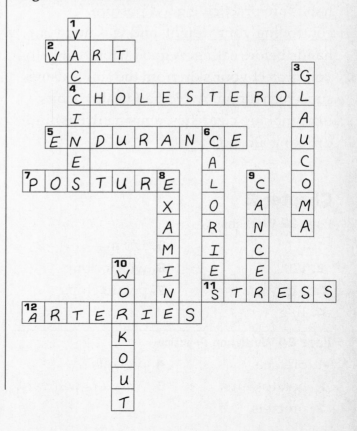

## Chapter 5

**Page 52 Workshop**

1. Jesse C. Rivera, her son
2. Central Animal Hospital
3. He slipped on a wet floor and turned his ankle.
4. All American Insurance

**Page 54 Workshop Practice**

The answers on the form will vary. Print clearly and fill out the form completely.

**Pages 54–55 Comprehension**

1. Friends can tell you about doctors they like. You can call a nearby hospital or your insurance company and ask them to suggest a doctor.
2. People need hospitalization, medical, and major medical insurance.
3. Many people buy group health insurance because group plans cost less than private plans and may be provided through the company where the people work.
4. Many people join an HMO to pay less for health care. Members pay a fee to join the HMO and get a special rate for medical care—doctor visits, surgery, and hospital stays.
5. Medicare is a government health insurance program for people 65 and older. Medicaid is another government health insurance program for people with low incomes.

**Page 55 Vocabulary**

1. family practitioner
2. specialist
3. Hospitalization
4. Major medical
5. surgeon

## Chapter 6

**Page 61 Workshop**

1. Take 1 tablet 4 times daily.
2. penicillin
3. Take medication on an empty stomach 1 hour before or 2 to 3 hours after a meal. Finish all the medication unless otherwise directed by the doctor.

**Page 62 Workshop**

1. Any one of the following is correct: simple headache; minor muscular aches; minor aches and pains associated with bursitis, neuralgia, sprains, overexertion, menstrual cramps; the discomfort of fever due to colds and flu; temporary relief of minor aches and pains of arthritis and rheumatism.
2. 1 to 2 tablets 3 or 4 times daily
3. 1/2 to 1 tablet 3 or 4 times daily
4. Consult a physician.
5. no more than 3 days

**Page 63 Workshop Practice**

1. Take 1 tablet twice daily with plenty of water.
2. Sulfatrim
3. no
4. Finish all this medication unless otherwise directed by the doctor. Avoid prolonged or excessive exposure to direct and/or artificial sunlight while taking the medication. Take with plenty of water.

**Page 64 Comprehension**

You need a prescription from a doctor to buy an <u>antibiotic</u>. Antibiotics can cure diseases caused by <u>bacteria</u>. Antibiotics cannot cure illnesses caused by <u>viruses</u>. Prescription drugs are used to treat illnesses like <u>glaucoma</u> and <u>asthma</u>. Follow the <u>directions</u> on the labels of all medicines. Never drink <u>alcohol</u> while using any kind of medicine.

## Page **64** Vocabulary

**1.** d      **3.** b

**2.** a      **4.** c

## Chapter 7

### Page **72** Workshop

**1.** Sue Wong, her mother

**2.** American Health Insurance

**3.** It gives her a rash.

**4.** acetaminophen

### Page **74** Workshop Practice

The answers on the form will vary. Print clearly and fill out the form completely.

### Pages **74–75** Comprehension

**1.** common cold and ear infection

**2.** do rescue breathing

**3.** sore throat

**4.** rabies

**5.** latex gloves

### Page **75** Vocabulary

Answers will vary. You may use more than one vocabulary word in a sentence.

## Chapter 8

### Page **83** Workshop

**1.** anyone who has asthma, glaucoma, emphysema, chronic pulmonary disease, shortness of breath, difficulty in breathing or difficulty in urination due to enlargement of the prostate gland

**2.** excitability, especially in children; drowsiness

**3.** driving a motor vehicle or operating machinery or drinking alcoholic beverages

**4.** seek professional assistance or contact a Poison Control Center immediately

### Page **84** Workshop Practice

**1.** It can cause eye and skin irritation on contact. It may cause respiratory tract irritation if inhaled or be harmful if swallowed.

**2.** Flush immediately with large amounts of water, especially under eyelids.

**3.** Move to fresh air or seek medical attention if trouble continues.

### Pages **84–85** Vocabulary

**1.** drowsiness      **4.** fumes

**2.** unconscious      **5.** fuse

**3.** detergents

### Page **85** Comprehension

**1.** True

**2.** True

**3.** False; It is dangerous to wear headphones when riding a bike.

**4.** True

**5.** False; Keep your windows open when using paint and paint thinners.

### Page **87** Crossword Puzzle

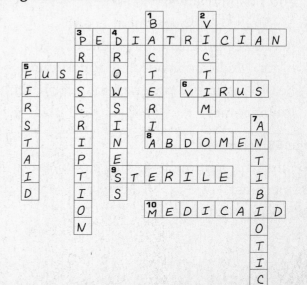